Timely Words

Inspiration for Everyday Life

"How delightful is a timely word!"
(Proverbs 15:23)

Gene Jennings

Late Night Press
North Augusta, S. C.

ISBN 0-9710120-0-8

First Printing, October 2002

Cover photos by Brook Facey

For additional copies of this book go to
www.timelywords.com
or by write to:
Late Night Press
1203 Crestview Drive
North Augusta, SC 29841

Printed in the U.S.A. by
Morris Publishing
3212 East Highway 30
Kearney, NE 68847
1-800-650-7888

In memory of Virginia Jennings,
a godly mother who always enjoyed a timely word.

Table of Contents

Foreword

When I felt God leading me toward the ministry of preaching and teaching, I knew that I would need a lot of help. One of the many ways that I have received help is by collecting stories, quotes, facts, and jokes that help illustrate a message. I noticed early in my preaching experience that most people remember the inspirational stories or funny jokes more than the actual teaching points. I've learned that great speakers are often great storytellers. Jesus drew large audiences with his ability to craft a story into a life-changing principle.

A career change actually led to *Timely Words*. Having moved away from the pulpit to a secular business, I wanted to continue to communicate Biblical principles to others. *Timely Words* began as a weekly newsletter distributed to my work associates every Thursday morning. Only a couple of weeks into this new venture, I learned that co-workers were faxing and copying *Timely Words* for their friends. On the occasional busy week when I didn't publish an edition, I received calls from devoted readers demanding to know the whereabouts of their weekly source of encouragement. I knew I was on to something.

What you hold in your hands is a compilation of *Timely Words* newsletter items. I am sorry to say that I cannot identify a source for all of the entries. The material was gathered from a variety of sources: books, magazines, newspapers, newsletters, emails, websites, friends, family, and fellow pastors. While some items are original most are taken from one of these other sources. Credit is given where possible.

Thanks to my family. You've always supported my endeavors - even when they seemed like crazy ideas. Thanks to my church, Stevens Creek Community Church. Thank you, Cliff and Bailey, my two offspring who add spice to my life. Most of all, thanks to my wife and best friend, Beth, who shows great love and patience for her husband, the night owl.

Gene Jennings

Timely Words

For

Your Soul

The Simple Life

An American investment banker was at the pier of a small coastal Mexican village when a little boat with one fisherman docked with a slim catch.

The American asked him, "Why didn't you stay out longer and catch more fish?"

The Mexican replied, "This is all I need to support my family for a few days."

"But what do you do with the rest of your time?" the American inquired.

"I sleep late, fish a little, play with my children, take siesta with my wife, Maria, stroll into the village each evening where I dine and play guitar with my amigos. I have a full and busy life."

The American scoffed at the Mexican. "Listen. I have an MBA from Harvard and I can help you. You should spend more time fishing and with the proceeds, buy a bigger boat. With the proceeds from the bigger boat, you could buy several boats, eventually you would have a fleet of fishing boats. Instead of selling your catch to a middleman, you would sell directly to the processor, eventually opening your own cannery. You would control the product, processing and distribution. You could leave this little village and move to Mexico City or even New York City where you will run your expanding enterprise."

"But how long will this take?" the fisherman asked.

"About 15-20 years," responded the expert.

"But what then?"

The American laughed. "That is the best part...when the time is right you would sell your company stock and become rich."

"Rich," the Mexican dreamed aloud. "Then what?"

The businessman said, "Then you could retire, move to a small coastal village and sleep late, fish a little, play with your grandkids, take siesta with your wife, stroll to the village in the evenings and play the guitar with your friends." (*FYI: Georgia News and Views*, June 1999)

"Show me, O Lord, my life's end and the number of my days; let me know how fleeting is my life." (Psalm 39:4)

Out of Focus

There is a legend that surrounds the Taj Mahal in India. The Taj Mahal is one of the architectural wonders of the world. The emperor and builder of this masterpiece was Shah Jahan who ruled from 1628-1658. His wife, known as Taj Mahal, died in 1631. The Shah was devastated. He resolved to honor her by constructing a temple that would serve as her tomb. The coffin was placed on a large piece of land and construction of the temple began around the coffin. No expense would be spared to make her final resting place magnificent.

The weeks turned into months and the months into years. It took 22 years and twenty thousand people to complete the project. The Shah's grief was overshadowed by his passion for the project. He no longer mourned her absence. The construction project consumed him. One day, while walking from one side of the construction site to the other, his leg bumped against an old, dusty, wooden box. While the prince, miffed at the ugly, dirty box, brushed the dust off his leg, he ordered a worker to throw the box out.

The Shah didn't know he had ordered the disposal of his wife's coffin that had been forgotten and hidden beneath layers of dust and time. The one the temple was intended to honor was forgotten, but the temple was erected anyway.

How many times do we lose focus on the things that ought to be dear to us because of other pressing needs? Be careful that the urgent things don't always overshadow the important things in life.

A Dog, God, and Adversity

If you are walking a dog and the leash gets wrapped around a pole, the dog will continue running forward. This only causes the leash to tighten. Both the dog and the owner are after the same goal, but the owner must resist the dog by pulling him opposite the direction he wants to go. The master, sharing the same intention, but understanding better than the dog where he really wants to go, takes an action precisely opposite to that of the dog's will. It is in this way that God uses adversity.
(C. S. Lewis, *Mere Christianity*)

"We know that God causes all things to work together for good to those who love God, to those who are called according to His purpose." (Romans 8:28)

"God may conceal his purposes so that we will live on his promises."

"A smooth sea never made a skillful sailor."

"If things don't seem to be coming your way, perhaps you are on the wrong road."

A Good Book

Andrew Young, former mayor of Atlanta and U.S. Ambassador to the United Nations, urged the graduating class of the University of Maryland's Eastern Shore campus to "get a Bible" and read a chapter a day. "It won't hurt you at all," he said in his commencement address, "and it will give you more illumination and purpose in life. It's better to invest fifteen dollars in a Bible now than twenty-five dollars an hour for a psychiatrist later."

"I thoroughly believe in a university education for both men and women, but I believe a knowledge of the Bible without a college degree is more valuable than a college degree without the Bible." (William Lyon Phelps)

"Should all the people dust off their Bibles, we would have one of the greatest dust storms of all time."

"Your word is a lamp to my feet, and a light for my path." (Psalm 119:105)

Slow Anger

Dwight D. Eisenhower commanded an army and was president of the United States. But when Eisenhower was a child, he had an explosive temper.

Once when his parents did not let him do something with his older brothers, he flew into a rage. He ran outside and began pounding his fists into the trunk of an apple tree. The next thing he remembered was his father grabbing him, shaking him, whipping him, and sending him to his room without supper. Moments later his mother came in, washed and bandaged his hands, and then read Proverbs 16:32, "He that is slow to anger is better than the mighty."

At that moment Dwight Eisenhower made a decision that for the rest of his life he would control his anger and his anger would not control him. He claimed that lesson to be one of the most decisive moments of his life.

"My dear brothers, take note of this: Everyone should be quick to listen, slow to speak and slow to become angry..." (James 1:20)

One Way to Pray

Grandpa was going by his granddaughter's bedroom one night when he saw her kneeling beside her bed, head bowed, and hands folded, repeating the alphabet.

"What are you doing?" he asked her.

She explained, "I'm saying my prayers, but I couldn't think of just what I wanted to say. So I'm just saying all the letters, and God can put them together however He thinks best."

That's one way to pray! Maybe we could learn something from this little girl. We, too, need to trust God to show us how to pray.

When Jesus' disciples asked Him to teach them to pray, He gave them the model prayer. You probably know it as the Lord's Prayer. It is a model because it has all of the major components of what a prayer should include: praise, submission, petition (asking), and confession. If you haven't read it lately, you can find it in the New Testament, Matthew 6:9-13.

"Pray is one four-letter word you can use anywhere."

True Colors

Spectators watched a peacock spread its tail and show its bright feathers in a park zoo. The bird thrilled them as it strutted about in its pen, showing off its beautiful tail.

Then a duck waddled across the park. The peacock became angry and chased the duck into a pond. In its rage, the peacock's tail closed like a fan and it seemed ugly.

But the duck, swimming gracefully in the water, seemed attractive. Those who had praised the peacock now delighted in the duck.

Sometimes our true colors don't show until we are put in a pressure situation. When the heat comes your way, do you react like the peacock or the duck? (*Seeds From the Sower*)

"Pride goes before destruction, a haughty spirit before a fall." (Proverbs 16:18)

"When pride comes, then comes disgrace, but with humility comes wisdom." (Proverbs 11:2)

Wise Guy

A college student came home after his first semester excited about all that he had been learning. He told his dad, "I have learned a lot about life. For example, in my philosophy class I learned that God made many mistakes."

"Oh?" responded the dad. "What kind of mistakes did God make?"

Pointing to a watermelon and an acorn the wise student replied, "Do you see that big thing growing on a little vine and that little thing growing on a big tree? That's backwards. It should be the other way around."

Just then an acorn fell from a tree and hit the student on the head.

"Aren't you glad," asked his dad, "that wasn't a watermelon?"

Be thankful that God is all-wise, all-powerful, always present, and that He knows what is best. Trust Him and you will be triumphant in life.

"The Lord is a refuge for the oppressed, a stronghold in times of trouble. Those who know your name will trust in you, for you, Lord, have never forsaken those who seek you." (Psalm 9:9-10)

Humility

Humble people don't think less of themselves – they just think about themselves less.

Influence

A minister was making a wooden trellis to support a climbing vine. As he was pounding away, a little boy walked up behind him to watch. The preacher was proud to know the young man was admiring his work. A few minutes later, the preacher said, "Well, son, trying to pick up some points on carpentry?"

"No," replied the boy. "I'm just waiting to hear what a preacher says when he hits his thumb with a hammer."

Be careful because you never know who might be watching you, or why.

"There is never a man so poor or unknown that he does not have an audience."

Bullseye Everytime

Police investigators were studying the work of what appeared to be a sharpshooter. They were amazed to find many bullseyes drawn around town with bullets that had penetrated the exact center of the targets. When they finally found the man who had been doing the shooting, they asked him about the technique he used to attain such accuracy. The answer was simple. He shot the bullet first, and drew the bullseye later.

You've probably done something like that before. Have you ever had a things-to-do list that seemed to overwhelm you? Then you did something that wasn't on the original list and you wrote it down so that you could immediately scratch it off?

The Bible advises us to set goals and make plans. Proverbs 16:3 says, "Commit to the Lord whatever you do, and your plans will succeed."

"The reason some people are successful is that they put work and plans together."

Strong Possibilities

Al was sick emotionally and physically. He entered school two years late, but stayed just three months. The authorities felt he was confused.

His mother tried teaching him, but he learned so fast that she gave up. When he was nine years old, she gave him a chemistry book. Playing with chemicals he burned down his father's barn, and three years later a baggage car.

This deaf boy, Thomas Alva Edison, who was considered backward, became one of the world's greatest inventors.

It's possible to turn obstacles into opportunities. The Bible says that as we release our lives into the Lord's hands, we become much more than anyone might imagine. Philippians 4:13 says, "I can do all things through Christ who strengthens me". (*Seeds from the Sower*, Vol. 19, No. 7)

Your Dash

What are you doing with your dash? No, not the dashboard on your car. The dash between your birth year and your death year. One day there will be a headstone with your name on it in a cemetery. It will have your name and the beginning and ending years of your life. In between, there will be a dash. The dash may represent 80 years or more. Regardless of the years represented, the question remains, "What are you doing with your dash?"

Are you accomplishing your purpose in life? Do you have one? Are you making a life or making a living? Are you leaving a positive impression on those around you or are you leaving them in depression?

These are hard questions yet it is a hard reality. Consider the life of King David of Old Testament fame. The Bible simply says that "when David had served God's purpose in his own generation, he fell asleep," (i.e. he died). You have a purpose for your generation. How are you doing with your dash?

If It Feels Good Do It

A man sat waiting for the light to turn green when his car was rear-ended. The two drivers hopped out of their cars and a vicious argument ensued. The man at fault defended himself by saying, "I really felt like running into someone today to vent my frustrations, and your bumper sticker has given me license to crash into your car." The bumper sticker read: "If it feels good, do it."

One of the problems with the world today is that too many people are looking out for number one instead of looking out for each other.

The Right Perspective

A businessman had an angel come to visit him who promised to grant him one request. The man requested a copy of *The New York Times* for one year in the future. As he was studying the future prices on the New York Stock Exchange, he boasted of his plans and the increased riches that would be his as a result of this "insider" look into the future.

He then glanced across the newspaper page only to see his own name in the obituary column. Obviously, in the light of his certain death, money was no longer important.

"Teach us to number our days aright, that we may gain a heart of wisdom." (Psalm 90:12)

A Breakdown on Pride

P - I am concerned with my *position.*
R - I want my *rights.*
I - I am most *important.*
D - My *desires* are more important than yours.
E - I *expect* everyone to agree with me.

Jesus said, "Whoever exalts himself will be humbled, and whoever humbles himself will be exalted." (Matthew 23:12)

Great Wall of Integrity?

In ancient China, the people desired security from the barbaric tribes to the north. So they built the Great Wall of China. It was too high to climb over, too thick to break down, and too long to go around. Security was achieved or so it seemed.

The only problem was that during the first hundred years of the wall's existence, China was invaded three times. Was the wall a failure? Not really – for not once did barbarians climb over the wall, break it down, or go around it.

How then did they get into China? The answer lies in human nature. They simply bribed a gatekeeper and then marched right in through a gate. The fatal flaw in the Chinese defense was placing too much reliance on a wall and not putting enough effort into building character into the gatekeeper.

"The man of integrity walks securely, but he who takes crooked paths will be found out." (Proverbs 10:9)

Hidden Hypocrisy

In any great forest you will find many huge trees. They tower above other trees and appear to be the very picture of strength and maturity. However, loggers will sometimes not even bother to cut down these huge trees. At first one wonders, "Why leave them? After all, a tree that big must contain twice or three times the amount of lumber as a smaller tree."

The reason is simple. Huge trees are often rotten on the inside. They are the hollow trees where animals like raccoons live. They are the trees that are often blown over in a strong windstorm because, while they appear to be the picture of strength, in fact their hollowness makes them weak.

This is the essence of hypocrisy – appearing strong on the outside but hollow and rotten on the inside.
"Therefore, rid yourselves of all malice and all deceit, hypocrisy, envy, and slander of every kind." (1 Peter 2:1)

The Jam Jar

Several years ago, *Decision* magazine published a story about a family who once received a jar of jam from some friends. Written on top of the jar was a note that read, "Do not open unless you're in a jam."

On the occasion when the family had a financial crisis, they opened the jar. Taped inside the lid was $1000 and another note. This note read, "Hopefully, this money will help you get out of your jam. When you find yourself out of this jam and able to do so, please replace this money and pass it on to someone else who might have need."

What a great way to be a blessing!

Moody on Giving

The great evangelist, Dwight L. Moody, understood how important money was to having an effective ministry and he wasn't timid about expressing it either. He had gone to a certain Mr. Farwell time and time again and once came back for another ten thousand dollar contribution.

"Mr. Moody," asked Farwell, "Must you always be coming to me for money?"

Moody replied, "Mr. Farwell, you grew up on a farm just like me. Isn't that correct?"

"Yes," Farwell agreed.

"Sir," Moody continued, "Did you ever take a pail to a dry cow?"

Do your givin'
While you're livin'
Then you're knowin'
Where it's goin'.

"It is more blessed to give than to receive." (Acts 20:35)

"A gift opens the way for the giver and ushers him into the presence of the great." (Proverbs 18:16)

Flawless

The pride and joy of a wealthy Englishman was a Rolls-Royce coupe that he had owned for years without any problems. One day, while driving down a bumpy road, his car hit a deep pothole, resulting in a broken rear axle.

The owner had the car shipped back to the Rolls plant in England and was surprised by the quick repair that was performed. He received no bill for the work and, knowing his warranty had run out, he had expected one. He waited for months and still no bill came. So he finally communicated with the company about the bill for his car repairs. Again the response from the factory was immediate. The reply said, "We have thoroughly searched our files and find no record of a Rolls-Royce axle ever breaking."

This is a case where the integrity and excellence of that company would not permit a flaw in workmanship to be made known. Similarly, Christ's sacrifice on our behalf was made so that our flaws would not be made known to the Father.

Teamwork

When geese migrate they can be seen flying in a V-shaped formation. While to us on the ground it is a thing of beauty, to the geese it is an essential for survival. If you watch them, you will observe that at certain intervals, relative to the strength of the headwind, the lead bird – who was doing most of the work by breaking the force of wind – will drop off and fly at the end of the formation.

The reason for this is that the V-formation is much more efficient than flying close, up to 60 percent less work is required. It has been discovered that the flapping wings create an uplift of air, an effect that is greater at the rear of the formation. So the geese take turns "uplifting" one another. By cooperating, the geese can achieve long migrations that would otherwise be exceedingly difficult for the strongest and deadly for the others.

When we "uplift" one another, we can go further than if we attempt life on our own.

Clear Perspective

A man and his wife were on a trip and stopped at a full-service gas station. After the attendant had washed their car's windshield, the man in the car said to the attendant, "It's still dirty. Wash it again."

So the gas station attendant complied. After washing it again, the man in the car angrily responded, "It's still dirty. Don't you know how to wash a windshield?"

Just then the man's wife reached over, removed her husband's glasses from his face, and cleaned them with a tissue. Then he put them back on and behold – the windshield was clean!

Our attitude has a great deal to do with how we look at things. The whole world can appear pretty bleak if we have a bad attitude. But when viewed with a positive attitude, the world seems bright and full of hope.

"The longer I live the more convinced I become that life is 10 percent what happens to us and 90 percent how we respond to it." (Charles R. Swindoll)

Tools of Friendship

A new homeowner's lawn mower had broken down. He had been working on it fruitlessly for two hours trying to get it back together. Suddenly, one of his neighbors appeared with a handful of tools.

"Can I help?" he asked. In twenty minutes he had the mower functioning beautifully.

"Thanks a million," the elated newcomer said. "And say, what do you make with such fine tools?"

"Mostly friends," the neighbor smiled. "I'm available anytime."

"A friend loves at all times, and a brother is born for adversity." (Proverbs 17:17)

"A man of many companions may come to ruin, but there is a friend who sticks closer than a brother." (Proverbs 18:24)

"A true friend walks in when the rest of the world walks out."

"Life is to be fortified by many friendships. To love, and to be loved, is the greatest happiness of existence." (Sidney Smith)

Forgiveness

A man who was telling his friend about an argument he'd had with his wife commented, "I hate it. Every time we have an argument, my wife gets historical."

The friend replied, "You mean hysterical."

"No," he insisted. "I mean historical. Every time we argue she drags up everything from the past and holds it against me!"

A man named John Oglethorpe, in talking to the famous preacher, John Wesley, once made the comment, "I never forgive."

Mr. Wesley replied, "Then, sir, I hope that you never sin."

"For if you forgive men when they sin against you, your heavenly Father will also forgive you. But if you do not forgive men their sins, your Father will not forgive your sins." (Matthew 6:14,15)

A Wasted Life

Pastor Ray Stedman tells of an occasion when he met a man who had just become a Christian at a Billy Graham crusade. The pastor encouraged him regarding his decision and mentioned, among other things, that he was free from the fear of death.

The man looked at Stedman and responded, "I've never feared death too much. But what I am afraid of is that I'll waste my life." (Ray Stedman, *Authentic Christianity*)

Flying and Faith

The degree of faith that one places in a given object is directly proportional to one's knowledge of the object. For example, consider a man terrified of flying. When he first arrives at an airport he buys flight insurance at a coin-operated insurance policy machine. He has his seat belt buckled twenty minutes before take-off and is sure to listen carefully to the routine emergency instructions given by the stewardess. He has no faith in the ability of the plane to get him to his destination. But, as the journey progresses, this passenger begins to change. He first unbuckles his seat belt, then has some lunch, and pretty soon is talking to the person next to him and joking.

Why the change? What happened? Is there more faith at 36,000 feet? Of course not. The more he learned about the object of faith, the plane, the more faith he exercised in that object.

So it is with us. The more we learn about the Lord, the more faith we can place in Him.

The Failed Genius

In 1879, a child was born to a poor Jewish merchant. In early life the boy suffered a haunting sense of inferiority because of the anti-Semitic feeling he encountered on every hand. Shy and introspective, the boy was so slow in learning that his parents had him examined by specialists to see if he was normal. In 1895, he failed his entrance exam at the Polytechnicum in Zurich, Switzerland, though a year later he tried again and succeeded. Later he received a doctorate from the University of Zurich, yet obtained only an obscure job as a patent examiner in a patent office.

Who was he? The man who formulated the theory of relativity, Albert Einstein, one of the greatest geniuses who ever lived. He never let early failures defeat him.

Timely Thought

"Show me your ways, O Lord, teach me your paths; guide me in your truth and teach me, for you are God my Savior, and my hope is in you all day long." (Psalm 25:4,5)

The Benefits of Silence

People love noise. Why? Probably because we do not like to stop and think. What would it be like if all radios, tape players, stereos, and televisions stopped working? Trembling hands would immediately twirl dials, adjust knobs, and flip switches. Eyes would be dilated with the fear of silence. People would be running the streets in terror.

Incessant noise is like a narcotic for modern man. People will listen to anything to avoid silence. Why else do we have so many talk shows, round-the-clock news shows, sporting events, tapes, CD's, etc.? Noise blocks out the despairing cry of our own souls, as well as the still, small voice of God. Perhaps we would be wise to occasionally take God's hand and journey into the land of silence.

Richard Foster in his book, *Celebration of Discipline*, said, "In contemporary society our Adversary majors in three things: noise, hurry, and crowds. If he can keep us engaged in 'muchness' and 'manyness,' he will rest satisfied."

"Be still and know that I am God. I will be exalted among the nations, I will be exalted in the earth." (Psalm 46:10)

Friendly Influence

A Peanuts cartoon showed Peppermint Patty talking to Charlie Brown. She said, "Guess what, Chuck? The first day of school, and I got sent to the principal's office. It was your fault, Chuck."

"My fault?" he responded. "How could it be my fault? Why do you say everything is my fault?"

"You're my friend, aren't you?" she said. "You should have been a better influence on me."

While Peppermint Patty was seeking to pass the buck, she was in a very real sense right. We should be a good influence on our friends. We certainly do have an influence on everyone we encounter, whether for good or for bad. In Matthew 5:16,

Jesus said, "Let your light shine before men, that they may see your good deeds and praise your Father in heaven." (Andy Hunter in *The Mission*, September 12, 1999)

Timely Thoughts

"Your work is a portrait of yourself."

"Friendship is the act of giving, not getting."

"In every triumph there's a lot of try."

"Don't live in a worry."

From Trials to Triumphs

One morning a man saw his home and business washed away by a flood. Dazed and distressed, he stumbled onto a shining object the water had washed there. It was gold. The flood which had made him penniless made him wealthy.

Oftentimes our trials become our triumphs. John Bunyan was cast in prison. While in prison he wrote *Pilgrim's Progress*. His adversity became an opportunity to honor God and help mankind. (*Seeds From The Sower*, Vol. 19, No. 10)

Simple Contentment

"For we brought nothing into the world, and we can take nothing out of it. But if we have food and clothing we will be content with that. People who want to get rich fall into temptation and a trap and into many foolish and harmful desires that plunge men into ruin and destruction. For the love of money is a root of all kinds of evil. Some people, eager for money, have pierced themselves with many griefs." (1 Timothy 6:7-10)

Miraculous Courage

"Christy Brown," reported *The London Times*, "has typed a wonderful novel with the little toe of his left foot." Brown, the story continued, didn't type the novel with his toe as a publicity stunt. It is the only way he can communicate.

Brain-damaged at birth, unable to walk, talk, or feed himself, his story is a miracle of human courage.

Faith that's practiced doesn't perish. Hope that's exercised doesn't evaporate. Courage that's genuine doesn't give up.

The apostle Paul wrote, "God's grace is sufficient for you, for His power is made perfect in weakness." (*Seeds from the Sower*)

Timely Thoughts

"Hope is a good thing – maybe the best thing, and no good thing ever dies." (Stephen King, *The Shawshank Redemption*)

"The human body was designed to walk, run or stop; it wasn't built for coasting." (Cullen Hightower)

Throwing Rocks

When is it good to have rocks thrown at you? A boy's toy boat went out of reach on a pond and started floating away. A man on the other side of the pond started throwing rocks at the boat. The boy became horrified at what might happen. But then he realized that the rocks were creating ripples that finally pushed the boat back toward the shore and into the boy's hands.

Many times it appears that life is throwing rocks at us. But it may be that our circumstances are being used to bring us back home.

Creative Deception

A woman who had acquired wealth and social prominence decided to have a book written about her genealogy. The author she engaged for the assignment discovered that one of her uncles was a murderer who had been electrocuted in prison. When the author insisted that this must be included in the book, the woman pleaded that he find a way of saying it that would hide the truth.

When the book was published, the section about this particular uncle read as follows:

"One of her uncles occupied the chair of applied electricity in one of America's best known institutions. He was very much attached to his position and literally died in the harness."

"The Lord detests lying lips, but he delights in men who are truthful." (Proverbs 12:22)

True Freedom

Many people think that freedom is the license to do whatever a person wants, but true freedom is the ability to do what is right. It takes obedience in order to have true freedom. I can sit at a piano and be at liberty to play any keys that I want, but I don't have freedom, because I can't play anything but noise. I have no freedom to play Bach or even "Chopsticks." Why? Because it takes years of practice and obedience to lesson plans to be truly free at the piano. Then, and only then, does one have the freedom to play any piece of music.

The same is true of freedom in living. To be truly free, we must have the power and ability to be obedient.

"You, my brothers, were called to be free. But do not use your freedom to indulge the sinful nature; rather, serve one another in love." (Galatians 5:13)

"The sweetest freedom is an honest heart."

"He who has lost his freedom has nothing else to lose." (German proverb)

Faith Thoughts

Faith is central to all of life. For example, you go to a doctor whose name you cannot pronounce and whose degrees you have never verified. He gives you a prescription you cannot read. You take it to a pharmacist you have never seen before. He gives you a chemical compound you do not understand. Then you go home and take the pill according to the instructions on the bottle. All in trusting, sincere faith!

At a burning building in New York City, a blind girl was perched on the fourth-floor window. The firemen had become desperate. They couldn't fit the ladder truck between the buildings, and they couldn't get her to jump into a net, which she, of course, could not see.

Finally her father arrived and shouted through the bullhorn that there was a net and that she was to jump on his command.

The girl jumped and was so completely relaxed that she did not break a bone or even strain a muscle in the four-story fall.
Because she trusted her father completely, when she heard her father's voice she did what he said was best.

"We walk by faith, not by sight." (2 Corinthians 5:7)

"The righteous will live by his faith." (Habakkuk 2:4)

"The business of faith is to believe things that are out of sight."

Awesome!

A single human chromosome contains twenty billion bits of information. How much information is twenty billion bits? What would be its equivalent, if it were written down in an ordinary printed book in modern human language?
   Twenty billion bits are the equivalent of about three billion letters. If there are approximately six letters in an average word, the information content of a human chromosome corresponds to about five hundred million words. If there are about three hundred words on an ordinary page of printed type, this corresponds to about two million pages. If a typical book contains five hundred such pages, the information content of a single human chromosome corresponds to some four thousand volumes. It is clear, then, that the chromosome contains an enormous library of information. (Carl Sagan, *The Dragons of Eden*)

"I praise you because I am fearfully and wonderfully made; your works are wonderful, I know that full well." (Psalm 139:14)

Amazing Grace

"When I get to heaven, I shall see three wonders there: The first wonder will be to see many there whom I did not expect to see; the second wonder will be to miss many people whom I did expect to see; the third and greatest of all will be to find myself there." (John Newton, author of "Amazing Grace")

Selfish Prayer

A teenage girl was praying, "Lord, I'm not going to pray for myself today. I'm going to pray for others."

But at the end of her prayer she added, "And give my mother a handsome, rich son-in-law."

It's hard not to be selfish in our prayers. But praying for others is one of the greatest things we can do.

Someone once asked G. Campbell Morgan, a famous British preacher, "Do you think we ought to pray about even the little things in life?"

Dr. Morgan replied, "Can you think of anything in your life that is big to God?"

Worry

In a *Peanuts* comic strip, Linus said to Charlie Brown, "I guess it's wrong to be worrying about tomorrow. Maybe we should think only about today."

"No," answered Charlie Brown, "that's giving up! I'm still hoping that yesterday will get better."

There are two days we can't do anything about – yesterday with its mistakes and tomorrow with its mission. But we can ask for God's pardon for yesterday's faults and God's power for tomorrow's functions.

Jesus said in Matthew 6:34, "Don't be anxious about tomorrow. God will take care of your tomorrow. Today has enough troubles of its own." (*Seeds From the Sower*)

From Weakness to Strength

A teenage boy named Danny lost his left arm in a car wreck. He went to a judo master for therapy. He did well in judo classes. So well, in fact, that he signed up for a judo tournament.

The teacher taught the others many moves but he only concentrated on one specific move with Danny. Danny wondered why he did this, but he never questioned the judo master.

Danny won three matches in the tournament. Then he faced the champ. Just when it seemed that he was about to lose, Danny used the move and won the tournament.

Danny asked the teacher, "How did you know I could win with that move?"

"Because," replied the master, "The only known defense for it is for your opponent to grab your left arm."

If you let him, God can take your weakness and make it your strength.

Thankful Thoughts

An evergreen tree is always green despite the changes in weather around it. It is green in the heat of summer as well as the cold of winter. Our lives are to be characterized by an enduring thankfulness that is unaffected by the changes around us. When the heat of a pressured week or the deadly cold of pain strikes us, we should stand "ever green," always thankful, regardless of that which surrounds us.

"Enter His gates with thanksgiving and His courts with praise; give thanks to Him and praise His name. For the Lord is good and His love endures forever; His faithfulness continues through all generations." (Psalm 100:4)

A little boy was asked by his father to say grace at the table. While the rest of the family waited, the boy eyed everything on his plate that his mom had prepared. After examining the meal, he bowed his head and said, "Lord, I don't like the looks of it, but I thank you for it and I'll eat it anyway. Amen."

Hands of Destiny

Have you ever attempted to share your dreams with someone only to have them spotlight all of the reasons why your dreams will never come true? You see the opportunity in a situation while they see the obstacles. You see the potential while they see the pitfalls. It reminds me of the classic "Peanuts" cartoon where Charlie Brown and Lucy are pictured standing together. Charlie Brown is holding his hands up in the air and looking at them with wonder. He says, "Lucy, these hands may, in fact, be the hands of destiny. These hands may someday build bridges. These very hands may someday perform lifesaving surgery.

Someday these hands may get the winning hit in the World Series game. Lucy, these hands are hands of destiny!"

Then in the final frame, as Charlie Brown is still looking at his hands in wonder, Lucy says, "You have jelly on your hands, Charlie Brown!"

There seems to be an overwhelming number of "Lucys" in the world – people who are always looking for reasons

something cannot or will not happen. In the Old Testament, Moses sent twelve spies to examine the Promised Land. Ten of the twelve spies returned in fear declaring that the obstacles of possessing the land were too great. The remaining two, Joshua and Caleb, came back with a different report. They said "we can certainly do it" (Numbers 13:30). All twelve of the spies saw the same situation, but only two of them saw the potential of victory. What made the difference? Joshua and Caleb refused to concentrate on the size of the enemy, but instead marveled at the size of their God. (Dr. Marty Baker, *Around the Creek*, September 1999)

The Truth About Death

In Las Vegas, a big-time gambler dies and a friend delivers the eulogy. "Tony isn't dead," the friend says. "He only sleeps."

A mourner in the back of the room jumps up. "I've got a hundred bucks that says he's dead!"

According to the Bible, the gambler's friend was correct. The Bible describes death as sleep. See Psalm 13:3; 1 Corinthians 15:6,17, 18,20,51.

A Christmas Story

And there were in the same country, children keeping watch over their stockings by the fireplace. And, lo, Santa Claus came upon them; and they were sore afraid. And Santa said unto them; "Fear not, for behold, I bring you good tidings of great joy which will be to all people who can afford it. For unto you will be given great feasts of turkey, dressing, and pies; and many presents; and this shall be a sign unto you, ye shall find the presents, wrapped in bright paper, lying beneath a tree adorned with tinsel, colored balls, and lights. And suddenly, there will be with you a multitude of relatives and friends, praising you and saying, 'Thank you so much, it was just what I wanted.'

And it shall come to pass as the friends and relatives have gone away unto their homes, the parents shall say to one another, 'Wow! What a mess to clean up! I'm too tired. Let's go to bed and pick it up tomorrow. Thank goodness Christmas only comes once a year!' And they go with haste to their beds."

Our Greatest Need

If our greatest need had been knowledge, God would have sent His Son as an educator.

If our greatest need had been money, God would have sent His Son as an economist.

If our greatest need had been pleasure, God would have sent His Son as an entertainer.

Our greatest need is salvation. So God sent His Son to be the Savior.

"He will be great and will be called the Son of the Most High." (Luke 1:32)

Going Nowhere

In *Alice in Wonderland*, at one point Alice says to the Chesire Cat, "Would you tell me, please, which way I ought to go from here?"

"That depends a good deal on where you want to get to," said the Cat.

"I don't much care," replied Alice.

"Then it doesn't matter which way you go," responded the Cat.

As with Alice, so it is with us. Without goals and objectives, we have nowhere to go and we'll just keep wandering aimlessly.

Many people make resolutions and goals. Goals give hope. Goals inspire and motivate. To wake up in the morning with a clear objective for the day adds so much more to life. To begin a day with no hope or inspiration makes for a long, dreary day.

The apostle Paul speaks of "pressing on toward the goal" in his New Testament letter to the Philippians (3:14). His goal was to be all that God wanted him to be. That's not a bad goal for each of us.

Homemade Miracles

Twelve ministers were on a commercial airline flight when they encountered an awful storm.   One of them told the flight attendant, "Tell the pilot everything will be okay because twelve ministers are on board."

The stewardess returned shortly after saying, "The pilot said he was glad to have twelve ministers aboard, but he'd rather have four good engines."

Jesus was a miracle worker.   He specialized in the supernatural. But he delighted in using men and things.

When he fed the five thousand, he used a young boy and a homemade lunch. Will you let him use you and what you have?

"As each one has received a special gift, employ it in serving one another, as good stewards of the manifold grace of God."   (1 Peter 4:10)

The Power to Overcome

Lord Nelson was Great Britain's greatest naval officer.   He defeated the combined French and Spanish fleets and established Britain's rule of the seas.

But Lord Nelson suffered from seasickness through his entire life. However, he didn't let it hinder him. He not only learned to live with it, but he learned to overcome it.   He conquered his sickness and learned to be a winner in spite of his weakness.

The apostle Paul had a weakness too. He called it his "thorn in the flesh."   Bible scholars aren't exactly sure what Paul's thorn was but Paul wrote that the thing he had learned through it was that God's grace was sufficient. In other words, God gave him the strength to carry on even with a handicap.

Follow Your Passions

Antonio wanted to make music more than anything else in the world. But his teacher said, "Your voice is too screechy to sing and your hands are too small to play the violin. Give it up."

But a friend named Amati told Antonio, "Music is in your heart. Give your life to God. He will give you the desires of your heart. Develop your talent. You can make music."

Antonio gave himself to God, and with God's help, he developed his talent. With that, Antonio Stradivarius became the greatest maker of violins in the world.

Give yourself to God and heartily strive for excellence in the work that God leads you to do! (*Seeds From The Sower*, Volume 20, Number 1)

"Plan for the future by taking a firm grip on the present."

"Look and plan ahead. It wasn't raining when Noah built the ark."

The End Result of Faith

"When you come to the end of everything you know and are faced with the darkness of the unknown, faith is knowing one of two things will happen. Either there will be something solid for you to stand on, or you will be taught how to fly." (Barbara J. Winter)

Got Success?

About one hundred years ago, when Gail Borden was crossing the Atlantic, two children died from drinking contaminated milk. Immediately he determined to make milk safe for shipboard use. He discovered condensed milk.

When Borden died, his tombstone bore this testimony: "I tried and failed. I tried again and again and succeeded."

Great men and women have failed. But they made failure their mentor, not their mortician. Anxious to serve, they succeeded.

To succeed in all things, work your tongue little, your hands much, your brains more, and your knees most.

"If the ax is dull and its edge unsharpened, more strength is needed but skill will bring success." (Ecclesiastes 10:10)

Quotable

"The spectacle of a nation praying is more awe-inspiring than the explosion of an atomic bomb. The force of prayer is greater than any possible combination of man-made or man-controlled powers because prayer is man's greatest means of tapping the infinite resources of God." (J. Edgar Hoover)

The Best Guide

A hunting guide was lost in the woods. "I thought you were the best guide in Minnesota," asked a man in the hunting party.

"I am," replied the guide. "But I think we're in Canada now."

Wherever you may be, the Lord can guide you from trouble to triumph. But between your will and His will there must be a blending, not a battling.

To know the Lord's will is important, but never enough. You must get into it and go on in it.

Out of His will there's no success. In His will there's no failure.

The Gift

A bus was bumping along a back road in the South. In one seat, an elderly gentleman sat holding a bunch of fresh flowers. Across the aisle sat a young girl whose eyes came back again and again to the man's flowers. The time came for the old man to get off. Impulsively he thrust the flowers into the girl's lap. "I can see you love the flowers," he explained, "and I think my wife would like for you to have them. I'll tell her I gave them to you."

The girl accepted the flowers, then watched the old man get off the bus and walk through the gate of a small cemetery. (Bennet Cerf)

If I Had My Life to Live Over
(Interviews with the elderly and terminally ill)

"I'd dare to make more mistakes."

"I'd relax. I would limber up."

"I would take more chances."

"I would take more trips."

"I would eat more ice cream and less beans."

"If I had it to do again, I would travel lighter next time."

"If I had my life to live over, I would start barefoot earlier in the spring and stay that way later in the fall."

"I would go to more dances."

"I would ride more merry-go-rounds."

"I would pick more daisies." (Jack Canfield and Mark Victor Hansen, *Chicken Soup for the Soul*)

"Teach us to number our days aright that we may gain a heart of wisdom." (Psalm 90:12)

Divine Settlement

An elderly woman had an older model car in excellent condition. She was hit by another car in a minor accident one day. The insurance company told her that, considering the car's age, they would give her a settlement on the damage. When the check arrived, she was unhappy with the low amount and went to see the insurance agent. Pulling out his desk drawer, he said, "I have a little blue book in here that says that's all your car is worth."

"Well," she replied, "I have a little black book at home that says, 'Thou shalt not steal.'"

She got a higher settlement.

Timely Thoughts

"The quality of a man's life is in direct proportion to his commitment to excellence, regardless of his chosen field of endeavor." (Vince Lombardi)

"Heaven is a great big hug that lasts forever." (Bill Keane, *Family Circus*)

The Rock

"The Lord is my rock, my fortress and my deliverer; my God is my rock, in whom I take refuge." (Psalm 18:2)

Burning Lesson

Earl Dickson married a lovely girl who couldn't cook. He found himself constantly bandaging her fingers when she burned them or cut them while preparing a meal.

Afraid that she might hurt herself when he wasn't there to help her, he began working on a protective bandage that was easy to apply and remove. In due time he came up with the "Band-Aid."

Oftentimes it takes some difficulty to bring about a great discovery. All sorrow and suffering are designed to teach a lesson we couldn't learn in any other way. The apostle Paul wrote "all things work together for good" to them who love the Lord.

Be aware that what is a difficulty in your life today could bring victory tomorrow.

Honk If You Don't Care

A lady's car stalled on a busy city street. As she tried to start the engine, the man behind her continuously honked his horn.

She got out of the car, walked to the man and said, "Sir, if you will start my car, I'll honk your horn."

It's easier to honk than to help isn't it? It's easier to complain than create. It's easier to find fault than to fix. But all of us have difficulties that distress us and problems that plague us. So let's give our sympathies genuinely, share our talents graciously, and serve God gladly.

That's what Jesus did. The Bible says He "went about doing good...for God was with Him" (Acts 10:38).

A Visit to the Top

Mike Wallace of CBS News was interviewing one of the Sherpa guides from Nepal who help climbers reach the top of Mount Everest. "Why do you do it?" Wallace asked.

"To help others do something they cannot do on their own," answered the guide.

"But there are so many risks, so many dangers," said Wallace. "Why do you insist on taking people to the top of the mountain?"

The guide smiled and said, "It is obvious that you have never been to the top."

Those who are willing to take risks are usually those who have a vision for their future. Like those who have been to the top of Mount Everest, risk takers know what it's like to reach the top – and they find that it's worth every drop of sweat when they do so.

The Bible indicates that faith is a risk worth taking and it is a wonderful feeling of satisfaction when we reach the top. Micah 4:2 says, "Let us go up to the mountain of the Lord...He will teach us his ways so that we may walk in his paths." (Andy Hunter, *The Mission*, March 12, 2000)

The Right Way

While traveling in an unfamiliar area, a tourist approached a sign that read, "Road Closed. Do Not Enter!" But the road ahead looked good, so he ignored the sign.

A few miles down the road he came to a bridge that had collapsed. He turned around and retraced the route. When he came back to the sign that he had ignored, he read on the other side, "Welcome Back, Stupid."

Many times our pride gets in the way and we think we know better than anyone else. What seems right or feels good often dictates our decision making. The wise thing is to recognize that there is a greater wisdom and higher authority when it comes to the issues of life. The Bible says, "There is a way that seems right to a man but in the end it leads to death" (Proverbs 14:12). Though our way may seem right all of the time, the right way to go is God's way. Seek His wisdom, for it is far greater than anything we might accomplish.

"True wisdom starts with a heart full of faith, not a head full of facts."

Food for Your Soul

"For if anyone thinks he is something when he is nothing, he deceives himself." (Galatians 6:3)

Thirsting for Faith

The story has been told of a man who was crossing a desert in the days of the pioneers. He ran into trouble and was dying of thirst when he spotted a pump near an abandoned shack. He had no water to prime the pump, but he noticed a jug of water near the pump with a note attached. It read, "There is just enough water in this jug to prime the pump, but not if you drink some first. This well has never gone dry, even in the worst of times. Pour the water in the top of the pump and pump the handle quickly. After you have had plenty to drink, refill this jug for the next man who comes along."

What would the man dying of thirst do? To follow the instructions and prime the pump without first taking a drink would be an exercise of faith. This is the kind of belief the Bible speaks of. Biblical belief requires that one stake his life on the truth of the promise. If the man follows the instructions, he takes the chance of pouring out all the water and getting none to drink if the pump fails. So he must trust that the message is right. He must act in belief, without first receiving, and must trust in the truth of the promise.

If God Approached Work Like We Do

In the beginning, it was nine o'clock, so God had to go to work. He filled out a requisition to separate light from darkness. He considered making stars to beautify the night, and planets to fill the skies, but thought it sounded like too much work; and besides, thought God, "That's not my job." So He decided to knock off early and call it a day. And He looked at what He had done and He said, "It'll have to do."

On the second day God separated the waters from the dry land. And He made all the dry land flat, plain, and functional, so that – behold – the whole earth looked like Idaho. He thought about making mountains and valleys and glaciers and jungles and forests, but He decided it wouldn't be worth the effort. And God looked at what He had done that day and said, "It'll have to do."

And God made a pigeon to fly in the air, and a carp to swim in the waters, and a cat to creep upon dry ground. And God thought about making millions of other species of all sizes and shapes and colors, but He couldn't drum up any enthusiasm for any other animals – in fact, He wasn't too crazy about the cat. Besides, it was almost time for the Late Show. So God looked at all He had done, and God said, "It'll have to do."

And at the end of the week, God was seriously burned out. So He breathed a sigh of relief and said, "Thank me, it's Friday."

Wise Words

"Teach us to number our days and recognize how few they are; help us to spend them as we should." (Psalm 90:12)

"It is better to take refuge in the Lord than to trust in man." (Psalm 118:8)

A Good Excuse?

I've been a sports fan all my life: football in the fall, basketball in the winter, and baseball in the spring and summer. But I'll never go to another game because they always ask me for money. The people I sat with weren't very friendly. The seats were too hard. The coach never asked my advice. The referee made some bad calls. Some people cared more about their looks than the game. Some games went into overtime and I was late getting home. The band played some numbers I didn't know. Too many games didn't fit into my schedule. My parents took me to too many games when I was growing up. I just read a book on sports and I know more than the coaches. I don't take my kids to any games so that they can make their own choices about what sport they like best.

Do you use the same excuses for not attending church? What keeps you from seeking God?

Timely Thought

"Above all else, guard your heart, for it is the well spring of life." (Proverbs 4:23)

Cattle Prayer

Shortly after Dallas Seminary was founded in 1924, it came to the point of bankruptcy. All the creditors were going to foreclose at noon on a particular day. That morning, the founders of the school met in the president's office to pray that God would provide. In that prayer meeting was Harry Ironside. When it was his turn to pray, he prayed in his characteristically refreshing manner: "Lord, we know the Bible says the cattle on a thousand hills are yours. Please sell some of them and send us the money."

While they were praying, a tall Texan came into the business office and said, "I just sold two carloads of cattle in Fort Worth. I've been trying to make a business deal go through and it won't work, and I feel that God is compelling me to give this money to the seminary. I don't know if you need it or not, but here's the check."

A secretary took the check and, knowing something of the financial seriousness of the hour, went to the door of the prayer meeting and timidly tapped. When she finally got a response, Dr. Lewis Chafer took the check out of her hand, and it was for the exact amount of the debt. When he looked at the signature, he recognized the name of the cattle rancher. Turning to Dr. Ironside, he said, "Harry, God sold the cattle!"

"At all times pray and do not lose heart." (Luke 18:1)

Worth Quoting

Opportunity knocks but once, but temptation leans on the doorbell.

The heaviest thing a person can carry is a grudge.

It is better to give others a piece of our heart than a piece of our mind.

Procrastination is the fertilizer that makes difficulties grow.

Happiness is found in helpfulness.

The first step to making your dreams come true is to wake up!

A hypocrite never intends to be what he pretends to be.

Good Favor

Who knows where a favor will lead?

Thomas Welch made grape juice in his kitchen, because his family didn't want to drink wine, and Welch's grape juice was born.

Elliot Handler turned out doll furniture for his friends, and he became the head of Mattel, one of the biggest toy companies in the world.

Margaret Rudkin baked bread in an old stove to satisfy her neighbor's craving for good bread, and Pepperidge Farm was born.

Today look for another's load to lift, another's problem to solve, another's desire to satisfy, and your favor may become your fortune. (*Seeds From the Sower*)

"Let us not lose heart in doing good, for in due time we shall reap if we do not grow weary. So then, while we have opportunity, let us do good to all men..." (Galatians 6:9,10)

"Do not be overcome by evil, but overcome evil with good." (Romans 12:21)

Couch Potatoes

Television sets in the U.S. are turned on an average of six hours a day. A Detroit newspaper offered 120 families $500 each to endure a month without watching TV. 93 families turned down the offer. The other 27 families reported that their lives significantly improved during the month without TV, but then they promptly returned to their former viewing habits.

The worst thing about TV is not what it puts into our mind so much as what it prevents us from doing. Watching TV kills intimacy and conversation and disrupts sustained thought. One therapist asked a family to write down the phrases most heard around the house over a two-week period. The two chart toppers were: "What's on?" and "Move." (John Ortberg, *The Life You've Always Wanted*)

"Therefore be careful how you walk, not as unwise men, but as wise, making the most of your time, because the days are evil." (Ephesians 5:15,16)

A Humble Visit

A few years ago, Queen Elizabeth made a visit to the United States. She brought along 4000 pounds of luggage including two outfits for every occasion, a mourning outfit in case someone died, 40 pints of plasma, and even leather toilet seat covers. She brought along her own hairdresser, two valets, and a host of attendants. When Queen Elizabeth visits another country, it easily costs some 20 million dollars.

In contrast to Queen Elizabeth's royal visits, God's visit 2000 years ago in Bethlehem took place in an animal shelter with no attendants present and nowhere to lay the newborn king but a trough. As a matter of fact, the birth of Christ, which is so significant that it divides history into B.C. and A.D., had more animal than human witnesses. Those human witnesses were "nobodies" - illiterate shepherds who were hired to watch the flocks of sheep owned by the wealthy. Shepherds who were restricted to the outer courtyard of the temple because they were considered "godless."

God came humbly to humble men and became known as "a friend to sinners."

Timely Thoughts

Of all the things you wear, your expression is the most important.

Shine like a light, but don't flash at people like lightning.

Lost time is never found.

A day ought to start with eager anticipation and end with pleasant memories.

The happiest people don't have the best of everything, they make the best of everything.

"Commit your works to the Lord and your plans will be established." (Proverbs 16:3)

Sailing Through Life

Life is a voyage. In the ninth chapter of the book of Job in the Old Testament, he wrote, "My years disappear like a swift ship." As we sail through life, we need:

A chart. Modern ships are equipped with radar, yet they carry a chart in case there are technical problems. Don't sail without the most reliable chart for life: the Bible. It's not a chart for an ancient mariner. It speaks to all ages at all times.

It is as relevant today as the latest self-help book. And much more reliable.

A captain. Consider letting the Lord on board your ship to steer you through both good and bad times. He doesn't promise immunity from trouble, but He does promise triumph. He doesn't guarantee good weather, but He does guarantee a safe landing. He doesn't promise that difficult times won't come, but He does promise that you will not be taken through any storms that you cannot endure. If you choose to sail with this Captain and His chart, you'll have an exciting journey.

A Good Word

"Be kind and compassionate to one another, forgiving each other, just as in Christ God forgave you." (Ephesians 4:32)

Missed Opportunity

The brother of a seminary student came to visit him one day. Unsure of directions, he turned to the first person who passed by and asked, "Is this Davidson Hall?" On hearing the man described later, the seminary student asked his brother if he had realized that he had been talking to a world-famous theologian. The brother couldn't believe it. He had the opportunity to ask any question – and he asked only where a building was.

Unfortunately that's how many of us pray. We talk to God and ask for silly little things that are really insignificant. Take the time and opportunity you have today to *really* talk to God.

"Devote yourselves to prayer, keeping alert in it with an attitude of thanksgiving." (Colossians 4:2)

The Greater Fool

A king said to his jester, "Here's my staff. When you find a greater fool than yourself, give it to him."

Years later the king was dying, and the jester came to see him. "I'm leaving soon," he confessed. "I'm going to another world."

"What preparation have you made?" asked the jester.

"None," moaned the king.

"Take this staff," said the jester. "You're a greater fool than I."

Think Your Day is Bad?

The average cost of rehabilitating a seal after the Exxon Valdez oil spill in Alaska was $80,000. At a special ceremony, two of the most expensively saved animals were released back into the wild amid cheers and applause from onlookers. A minute later they were both eaten by a killer whale.

In 1992, Frank Perkins of Los Angeles made an attempt on the world flagpole sitting record. Suffering from the flu, he came down eight hours short of the 400 day record. His sponsor had gone bust. His girlfriend had left him. And his phone and electricity had been cut off.

A woman came home to find her husband in the kitchen shaking frantically with what looked like a wire running from his waist towards the electric kettle.

Intending to jolt him away from the deadly current, she whacked him with a handy plank of wood by the back door, breaking his arm in two places. Until that moment, he had been happily listening to his Walkman.

Feel better?

"Do not worry about tomorrow, for tomorrow will care for itself. Each day has enough trouble of its own." (Matthew 6:34)

Perfect Timing

The world's stage was set for the birth of Christ at just the right time. Three influential groups shaped the world at the time. The Romans governed the world. The Greeks created the culture of the day and the Hebrews controlled religion. The Romans, with world domination on their minds, paved roads to allow for military maneuvers, trade, commerce and communication. The Greek world had a flexible language that allowed for the transmission of the good news of Christ to be communicated to thousands. The Hebrew world had established a monotheistic religion (i.e., there is but one God) and anticipated the coming of the Messiah.

The birth of Christ, at this particular time in world history, was no accident or coincidence. It was perfectly timed so that everyone possible might know about Immanuel, God with us. (Vance Havner)

"She will give birth to a son, and you are to give him the name Jesus, because he will save his people from their sins." (Matthew 1:21)

Ain't No Sense Worrying

Mickey Rivers, former Major League baseball player, stated his philosophy of life this way: "Ain't no sense worrying about things you got control over, because if you got control over them, ain't no sense worrying. And there ain't no sense worrying about things you got no control over either, because if you got no control over them, ain't no sense worrying." (*Dallas Morning News*, May 20, 1984)

"If God so arrays the grass in the field, which is alive today and tomorrow is thrown in the furnace, how much more will He clothe you, O men of little faith! Do not seek what you shall eat, and what you shall drink, and do not keep worrying." (Luke 12:28,29)

"Worry is like a rocking chair, it will give you something to do, but it won't get you anywhere."

"Ulcers are caused not by what you eat, but by what is eating you."

Walk the Walk

One day years ago, a crowd gathered at the Union Depot in Chicago to meet a Nobel Prize winner. He stepped off the train, thanked the crowd for coming, then ran to the side of an elderly woman who was carrying two heavy suitcases. The famous missionary doctor picked up her bags, took her to the bus, helped her on board and wished her well.

Dr. Albert Schweitzer apologized to the crowd for keeping them waiting so long. A reporter wrote, "This is the first time I ever saw a sermon walking."

Why don't you become a sermon in shoe leather? (*Seeds from the Sower*)

"Be kind to one another, tender hearted, forgiving each other, just as God in Christ also has forgiven you." (Ephesians 4:32)

"When you find someone without a smile, give them yours."

"Have a hand to give and a heart to forgive."

"Let's do it gets more done than do it."

Wouldn't Jenny Craig Be Easier?

A good diet: "Put a knife to your throat if you are a man of great appetite." (Proverbs 23:2)

Sign of Deception

A melon farmer's crop was disappearing fast from his field. Thieves were continually stealing the melons under the cover of the night. The farmer finally became desperate and in an attempt to save his crop from the vandals he decided to put up a sign.

The sign had on it a skull and crossbones, and it read, "One of these melons are poisoned." Only the farmer knew that it was not true.

Sure enough, for two nights not a melon was missing. But, after the third night, the farmer noticed that his sign had been altered. Someone had scratched out the word "one" and replaced it with another word so that the sign now read: "Two of these melons are poisoned."

Thinking to save his whole crop through deception, he lost it all, which just goes to illustrate Sir Walter Scott's observation: "Oh, what a tangled web we weave, when first we practice to deceive!"

"Those who cook up stories usually find themselves in hot water."

"A lie may take care of the present, but it has no future."

"Sometimes how well you sleep depends on how little you lie."

"A good memory is needed once you have lied."

Angelic Words

Rev. John Paton, a missionary in the New Hebrides Islands, told the story of an angelic encounter. Hostile natives surrounded his home one night, intent on burning out the Patons and killing them. John Paton and his wife prayed all during that terrifying night that God would deliver them. When daylight came, they were amazed to see the attackers leave for no particular reason.

One year later, the chief of the tribe became a Christian. Paton asked the chief what kept him and his men from burning down his house and killing his family. The chief replied in surprise, "Who were all those men you had there with you?" Paton replied, "There were no men there; just my wife and me." The chief argued that they had seen many men standing guard – hundreds of big men in shining garments with drawn swords in their hands. They circled the missionary house and the natives were afraid to attack.

Only then did John Paton realize that God had answered their prayers by sending his angels to protect them. (Billy Graham, *Angels: God's Secret Agents*)

Prayer Quotes

"Prayer is not grasping for things in the hand of God, it's grasping for the hand of God."

"It is not so true that 'prayer changes things' as that prayer changes me and I change things." (Oswald Chambers)

Discipline Works

Loose wires give out no musical tones, but when their ends are stretched and fastened, the piano, the harp, or the violin is born. Free steam drives no machine, but harnessed and confined with piston and turbine, it makes possible the great world of machinery. An unhampered river drives no generators, but dam it up and you can create sufficient power to light a great city. So our lives must be disciplined if we are to be of any real service in the world.

"The roughest road oftentimes goes straight to the top of the hill."

"Those who master themselves are able to master all things and all people."

"Lessons that are bitter to learn usually are sweet to know."

"Remember that it is the daily grind that gives a person polish."

"The fear of the Lord is the beginning of wisdom, but fools despise wisdom and discipline." (Proverbs 1:7)

Peace

There is a painting titled "Peace." It depicts waves crashing against jagged rocks. It portrays the violence of a crushing storm. It seems anything but peaceful. But down in a small corner of the painting, tucked away in the rocks, is a little bird sitting on her nest totally oblivious to the raging storm all about. That is peace.

"Great peace have they who love God's law, and nothing can make them stumble." (Psalm 119:165)

A Powerful Purpose

Author Calvin Miller writes of an antique wooden dynamite box he owns. The box was made in the 19th century. It was carefully constructed to withstand shock as its explosive contents were transported from the manufacturer to its place of use.

On the lid were large red and black letters that read, "DANGER DYNAMITE!" But Miller noted that the last time he saw the box, it was filled with a bunch of junk in his workshop.

Like the old antique dynamite box, we were created to transport God's power into the world. But if we are not careful we will clutter our lives with so many other things that we will lose the divine power that we were created to carry.

"For God has not given us a spirit of timidity, but of power and love and discipline." (2 Timothy 1:7)

"His (God's) divine power has given us everything we need for life and godliness through our knowledge of Him." (2 Peter 1:3)

A Critical Decision

The "Lady Be Good" was a massive bomber during World War II. She had flown many successful missions. On her last flight, she had pierced enemy air space, dropped her cargo of destruction and turned around to head home.

This night was different, however. As she reversed course for the return flight, she was pushed along by a powerful tail wind, causing her to travel much faster than normal. When the instruments told the pilots to land, they looked at their watches and knew that it was much too soon. They faced a critical decision. If they believed their instruments, they would come down out of the clouds and prepare to land. However, if they believed their watches, they would keep flying.

To come down too soon might expose them to enemy anti-aircraft fire. On the other hand, if they didn't come down immediately, and the instruments were right, they would overshoot the airfield, and perish in the desert, since they had no excess fuel. Life and death was in their hands. Do they trust their instruments or do they trust their own judgement?

They had to make a decision. They chose to ignore the instruments and believe their gut-level hunch. They stayed up. They overshot the airfield. Their plane was found days later, out of fuel, crashed in the desert. All crewmen had died.

In deciding where and when to land as our final destination, we must choose whether we look within ourselves for the answers, or whether we look outside ourselves, whether we trust our gut-level hunches, or whether we look for an instrument panel. The Bible is like an instrument panel. It tells us where we came from, where we are, and where we are going. It is up to us to decide whether or not to accept the "readings" we get from it.

Words of Wisdom

"Trust in the Lord with all your heart and do not lean on your own understanding. In all your ways acknowledge Him and He will make your paths straight. Do not be wise in your own eyes; fear the Lord and turn away from evil. It will be healing to your body and refreshment to your bones...How blessed is the man who finds wisdom and the man who gains understanding." (Proverbs 3:4-8,13)

Counting Worms

On a visit to East Texas, a Yankee planned a day of fishing. He stopped by a weather worn bait shop to prepare for the big day. A lanky, white-bearded Texan, clad in denims and a cowboy hat, waited on him.

"I'd like a dollar's worth of worms," the tourist said.

The Texan obliged him but as he was waiting on his order the Yankee began to worry that he might not have enough bait. "How many worms do you get for a dollar?" he asked the Texan.

"I'll do you right, son," he drawled. "Life's too short to be counting worms."

There's no time to concern ourselves with the trivial things of life. We ought to give ourselves to the higher things of life and encourage others to do the same.

"Seek first the kingdom of God and His righteousness..." (Matthew 6:33)

"The eye of the Lord is on those who fear Him, on those who hope for His lovingkindness." (Psalm 33:18)

Made to Stretch

God created man something on the order of a rubber band. A rubber band is made to stretch. When it is not being stretched, it is small and relaxed; but as long as it remains in that shape, it is not doing what it was made to do. When it stretches, it is enlarged; it becomes tense and dynamic, and it does what it was made to do. God created *you* to stretch. (Charles Paul Conn, *Making It Happen*)

"Consider it all joy, my brothers, when you encounter various trials, knowing that the testing of your faith produces endurance." (James 1:2,3)

"Trials can make a man bitter or better."

"Diamonds cannot be polished without friction. Neither can we be perfected without trials."

"Great trials often precede great triumphs."

"If it were not for the hot water, the tea kettle would not sing."

"He who has no clouds sees no rainbows."

Good Ole Days

In 1610, according to Witold Rybczynski in *Waiting for the Weekend*, the colonial legislature in Virginia adopted a three level series of penalties for failure to attend Sunday church services. One absence was punished with forfeiture of one week's provisions. Skipping church twice was punished by a whipping. The punishment for three unexcused absences was death.

Perhaps the legislature's intentions were good, but they missed the mark by a long shot. You can't legislate worship. Christianity is a *want to* faith, not a *have to* faith. God desires your worship to be from your heart. The Bible says God loves the praises of His people.

A Great Disaster

Did you ever fail so often you felt like giving up? Then listen to an experience of noted inventor Thomas Edison, who had only three months of formal schooling. In 1876, he opened a laboratory in Menlo Park, New Jersey. He enjoyed many successes there: a carbon transmitter on the telephone so that users no longer needed to shout, the phonograph, and the incandescent bulb. Then came the night his lab caught fire and burned to the ground. Edison stood there in the winter night, watching years of work go up in flames.

He suddenly called to his son (who grew up to become governor of New Jersey), "Charles, go find your mother. Bring her here. She'll never see anything like this as long as she lives!"

Did he say this in despair? The answer lies in a comment to his family the next morning: "There is great value in disaster.

All our mistakes are burned up. Thank God we can start anew."

"If any man is in Jesus Christ, he is a new creature; old things have passed away and all things become new." (2 Corinthians 5:17)

Persistent Peanut

Sparky failed every subject in the eighth grade and did poorly in high school. He wasn't good at sports, and he didn't fit in with the crowd. Sparky was a loser.

But he enjoyed drawing. He was proud of his artwork, but no one else was. He submitted cartoons to editors, but each one turned him down.

So he decided to write his autobiography in cartoons. He portrayed his childhood self – a little boy loser.

He created the comic strip "Peanuts," and today everyone likes Charlie Brown. Charles Schulz learned not to give up.

"The hen is the only one who can lay around and still be a producer."

"Weeds grow themselves – flowers need cultivation."

"Don't just entertain ideas, put them to work."

A Dirty Lesson

A parable is told of a farmer who owned a mule. The mule fell into an old dry well. The farmer heard the mule braying from the bottom of the well. After assessing the situation, the farmer decided that there was no way he could save the mule. He figured that the only humane way to take care of the mule would be to bury him. The farmer gathered his helpers together and they began hauling dirt to the mule's soon to be grave.

The mule went hysterical when he first realized what the men were doing. Then he figured out that every time he shook the dirt off of his back, he could step up on top of the dirt. Shake, step, shake, step, shake, step...the mule continued this process no matter how painful the heavy loads of dirt were or how distressing the situation. He refused to panic.

It wasn't too long before the old mule, battered and exhausted, stepped triumphantly over the wall of the well! What seemed like would bury him actually was a blessing to him. All because he learned how to handle his adversity.

For Richer

Three children returned home from a wedding and staged their own ceremony. The "bride" and the "groom" stood before the "minister" as he asked, "Do you take this man for richer or poorer?"

"For richer!" shouted the pretend bride.

You make your companion better or worse, stronger or weaker, richer or poorer by the life you live.

What greater thing is there for a man and woman, than to know that they are joined for life, to strengthen each other in their labor, to rest on each other in their sorrow, and to minister to each other in their pain.

That's taking each other "for richer." (*Seeds from the Sower*)

"The greatest thing a man can do for his children is love their mother."

"Abide in these three things, faith, hope, and love; but the greatest of these is love." (1 Corinthians 13:13)

Lunchroom Lesson

As the students entered the school cafeteria, they came to a bowl of apples. Above it was a sign written by one of the kitchen staff, "Take only one. Jesus is watching you."

As they were leaving the food line, they passed a bowl of cookies. Next to it was another sign, apparently written by a student, "Take as many cookies as you want. Jesus is busy watching the apples."

Some people are frightened to think that God is watching them. They think He is watching so that He can punish them for the things they do wrong. But the truth is that He watches so that He can help. The Bible says, "Let Him have all your worries for He's always watching everything that concerns you."

"Worry is the interest paid on trouble before it falls due."

"God is our refuge and strength, a very present help in trouble." (Psalm 46:1)

"Which of you by being anxious can add a single cubit to his life's span?" (Matthew 6:27)

When Life Gets Tangled

In a textile factory, a sign over the machines read, "When the threads get tangled, send for the foreman." One day the threads got tangled on one machine and the operator tried desperately to untangle them. Just then the foreman came along and asked, "Don't you see the sign?"

"Yes," was the reply, "but I'm doing my best to take care of it myself."

"Doing the best you can always means *sending for the foreman*," the foreman responded.

Doing our best with life's tangled problems means calling on the Great Overseer. (Vance Havner)

"Call on me in the day of trouble; I shall rescue you, and you will honor me." (Psalm 50:15)

Theology 101

The theological term used to describe God becoming man is incarnation. It can be illustrated this way:

Suppose you have an aquarium. You feed the fish daily. Every once in a while you clean the tank. When you go out of town, you drop a feeder in the aquarium so the fish will have plenty to eat while you're gone.

You would think with all the effort, concern, and money spent on the fish that they would be grateful. But if your hand gets close to them, they show one emotion: fear.

To your goldfish, you are deity. You are too large for them. Your actions are too incomprehensible. They see your acts of mercy and care as cruelty. The only way you could change their perception of you would be to become incarnate. You would have to become a fish and speak to them in a language they could understand.

A human being becoming a fish may seem a little far-fetched. (Actually, evolutionists believe we evolved from fish so they may not have a hard time with it!) God becoming a baby seems incredible. Yet that is exactly what happened that night in Bethlehem. God became a man so that we would know His love, grace, and mercy.

"The Word (God) became flesh and made His dwelling among us" (John 1:14).

A Matter of Time

A young employee had been arriving late for work every day. One morning his boss was waiting for him.

"Son," he said, "instead of giving you a gold watch when you retire, I'm going to give you this alarm clock now."

Time is one thing you can't recover. You can lose and recover money, but you can't lose and recover time. Time can't be redeemed so make good use of every moment you have. Others may have more talents or more money, but no one has more time. Each one of us has sixty minutes to the hour. Spend it wisely.

Successful Failure

In January 1993 near Alvin, Texas, 18 year-old Andrea Guereo and her brother came across a man who was slumped over the wheel of his truck and not breathing. Andrea administered CPR until an ambulance arrived to take the victim to a hospital, where he recovered.

Andrea was on her way home from a CPR certification exam, which she flunked. Andrea may have felt defeated after failing her CPR test. But when the real test came, she was a success.

There are many times in life when we feel like a failure because we don't meet certain standards that men have set. It is a blow to our self-esteem when we discover that we cannot be accepted because we do not qualify. However, when you consider your value in the eyes of God rather than the eyes of man, you will see that there is much reason for you to feel like a valuable person. God took special care to create you. Isaiah 64:8 says, "We are the clay, and you (God) are the potter. We are all formed by your hand."

Think about it. The very hand of God formed you. Still feel like a failure?

The Greatest Thing

"If I could speak in any language in heaven or on earth but didn't love others, I would only be making meaningless noise like a loud gong or a clanging cymbal. If I had the gift of prophecy, and if I knew all the mysteries of the future and knew everything about everything, but didn't love others, what good would I be? And if I had the gift of faith so that I could speak to a mountain and make it move, without love I would be no good to anybody. If I gave everything I have to the poor and even sacrificed my body, I could boast about it, but if I didn't love others, I would be of no value whatsoever.

Love is patient and kind. Love is not jealous or boastful or proud or rude. Love does not demand its own way. Love is not irritable, and it keeps no record of when it has been wronged. It is never glad about injustice but rejoices whenever the truth wins out. Love never gives up, never loses faith, is always hopeful, and endures every circumstance...There are three things that will endure – faith, hope, and love – and the greatest of these is love." (1 Corinthians 13:1-7,13)

Explaining God

Trying to explain God is like trying to explain a kiss. You can check the dictionary definition: "A caress with the lips; a gentle touch or contact."

But does that really capture the essence of what a kiss is? Does that describe what a mother does when she tenderly places her lips on the forehead of her newborn child? Is that what the young lover does when he says "good night" to his girl?

Just as words cannot completely capture all that is involved in what we know by experience and attempt to describe as a "kiss," we also cannot fully comprehend, explain, or define God. We can, however, know him through experiencing his revelation of himself to us in his Word and in the person of Jesus Christ.

"We know that the Son of God has come and has given us understanding, so that we might know the true God." (1 John 5:20)

"When Jesus came in the form of a servant, he was not disguising who God is. He was revealing who God is." (John Ortberg, *The Life You've Always Wanted*)

Thankfulness

Corrie Ten Boom, in *The Hiding Place*, relates an incident that taught her always to be thankful. She and her sister, Betsy, had just been transferred to the worst German prison camp they had experienced to that point. On entering the barracks, they found them extremely overcrowded and flea-infested.

That morning, their Bible reading in 1 Thessalonians had reminded them to rejoice always, pray constantly, and give thanks in all circumstances. Betsy told Corrie to stop and thank the Lord for every detail of their new living quarters. Corrie at first flatly refused to give thanks for the fleas, but Betsy persisted, and Corrie finally succumbed to her pleadings. During the months spent at that camp, they were surprised to find how openly they could hold Bible study and prayer meetings without interference from the German guards. It was not until later that they learned the reason the guards would not enter the barracks was because of the fleas.

Matthew Henry, a minister in the 18th century, wrote the following in his journal after being robbed: "Let me be thankful. First, because I was never robbed before. Second, because although they took my wallet, they did not take my life. Third, because although they took my all, it was not much. Fourth, because it was I who was robbed, not I who robbed."

First, Call Dad

While kayaking off the Isle of Wight in England, Mark Ashton-Smith, a 33-year-old lecturer at Cambridge University, capsized in treacherous waters. Clinging to his craft and reaching for his cell phone, Ashton-Smith's first inclination was to call his father. It didn't matter to the desperate son that his dad was training British troops in Dubai 3500 miles away. Without delay, the father relayed his son's mayday to the Coast Guard installation nearest to his son's location. Ironically, it was less than a mile away. Within 12 minutes, a helicopter retrieved the grateful son from the water.

When we are in peril, our first impulse should be to call our Father – the one we can trust to help us. (Greg Asimakoupoulos, *Leadership*, Spring 2002)

The Legend of the Cracked Pot

A servant in India had two large pots. The pots hung on each end of a pole that he carried across his back. One of the pots had a crack in it while the other pot was perfect and always arrived with a full portion of water at the end of the long walk from the stream to the master's house. The cracked pot arrived only half full.

For two years the man delivered only one and a half pots of water to his master's house. Of course, the perfect pot was proud of its accomplishments for it was achieving the very task in which it was created. The cracked pot was ashamed of its own imperfection and miserable that it was only able to accomplish half of what it was made to do. The cracked pot perceived itself to be a failure. It spoke to the waterman one day by the stream.

"I am ashamed of myself and I want to apologize to you."

"Why?" asked the servant. "What are you ashamed of?"

"I have been able to only deliver half my load because this crack in my side allows water to leak out all the way back to the master's house. Because of my flaws, you have to do all of this work and you don't get the full value from your efforts," the pot said.

The servant felt sorry for the cracked pot and in his compassion said, "As you return to the master's house, I want you to notice the beautiful flowers along the path."

As they went up the hill, the cracked pot noticed beautiful flowers on the side of the path. But at the end of the trail he felt bad again because he had lost half of his load.

The servant said to the cracked pot, "Did you notice that there are flowers on your side of the path but no flowers on the other side? That is because I have always known about your flaw and I used it for good. I planted flower seeds on your side of the path and every day while we walked back from the stream, you've watered them. For two years I've been able to pick beautiful flowers to decorate my master's table. Without you being just the way you are, he would not have this beauty to grace his house."

Each of us has our own unique flaws. But God can use our flaws to be a blessing to others. In God's economy, nothing goes to waste.

Timely Quotes

"Our problem is not that we desire too much but too little." (C.S. Lewis)

"Only those who risk going too far can possibly find out how far one can go." (T.S. Elliot)

"It will be gone before you know it. The fingerprints on the wall appear higher and higher. Then, suddenly, they disappear. (Dorothy Euslin)

"Each generation of the church in each setting has the responsibility of communicating the gospel in understandable terms, considering the language and thought forms of that setting." (Francis Schaeffer)

"I've reached one conclusion: If your name is on your dishes, then it's probably written in The Book too." (Valerie Fraser)

A Lasting Impression

A few years ago my daughter and I went with friends to the U.S. Open Tennis Tournament. Moments before the Ladies Championship final match began, they introduced the great women champions of yesteryear, from the oldest to the youngest.

These former champions were not introduced to just any crowd, but to enthusiastic New Yorkers! Yet, as the first elderly lady was escorted to center court, there were only a few polite claps from a handful of fans. Then as the announcer introduced the next one, the applause picked up a little. This continued, with each former star gaining an increment of more applause.

Finally they introduced someone whose name I recognized, and I joined in the applause. By the time they called Billie Jean King's name, the applause turned from polite to robust. But when they called out Chris Evert, the great lady of tennis, the stands went wild with thunderous approval!

As I sat in the stands observing this, I couldn't help but think how the first doddering old lady had been the Chris Evert of her year. But just fifty years later she was receiving only a few polite claps from a handful of fans. I wondered if she thought her significance would endure? And I wondered how many years it would be before Chris Evert was forgotten, worthy of only a few polite claps from a handful of courteous fans.

Memories are short. When we try to answer the question, "Who am I?" in terms of our fame and worldly accomplishments, we select an identity that will fade like sun-bleached furniture. (Patrick Morley, *The Man in the Mirror*)

Timely Words

For

Your Mind

A Burning Success

Two paddleboats left Memphis at about the same time to sail down the Mississippi River to New Orleans. As they traveled side by side, sailors from one vessel made a few remarks about the snail's pace of the other.

Words were exchanged. Challenges were made and the race began. Competition became vicious as the two boats roared through the Deep South.

One boat began falling behind. Not enough fuel. There had been plenty of coal for the trip, but not enough for a race. As the boat dropped back, an enterprising young sailor took some of the ship's cargo and tossed it into the ovens. When the sailors saw that the supplies burned as well as the coal, they fueled their boat with the material they had been assigned to transport. They ended up winning the race, but burned their cargo.

Be careful not to climb the ladder of success and wealth at the expense of your family, friends, and physical and spiritual welfare. (Max Lucado, *In The Eye of the Storm*)

Determination

Michael Jordan is known by all as one of the best basketball players of all time. It hasn't always been that way though. During his sophomore year in high school in Wilmington, NC, he didn't make the varsity team. Leroy Smith (who never made it to the NBA) beat out Michael Jordan for the only sophomore spot on the varsity squad. Jordan had to settle for the junior varsity team.

"He didn't sulk or threaten to quit. He just started working harder and improving his game," said his high school coach, Fred Lynch. "If anything, it made him more determined."

We shouldn't blame the coach, however. Leroy Smith was 6'7" at the time and Michael Jordan was only 5'10"!

Easy Street

From the island of Oahu comes a little Hawaiian wisdom. If you take the Pali Highway northbound out of Honolulu you will come to Pali Pass. At Pali Pass you can turn right on Park Street. Go one block on Park Street and you will arrive on Easy Street. Turn left on Easy Street and drive one block. You will then see a sign that reads, Dead End. (*Bits & Pieces*, November 14, 1991)

Vision: Just Do It

Phil Knight had a crazy idea in the early 1960's. He decided to sell imported running shoes from the back of his station wagon in Portland, Oregon. As an auditor, he was financially astute and figured he could make money by purchasing shoes from Japan and selling them in the U.S. His shoes were improved in the latter part of 1963 when he was joined in this venture by his college coach. Coach William Bowerman modified the imported shoes to make them better. Their start up investment was $1000. Today, Nike Inc. has a market value worth billions of dollars. When it comes to vision, "Just Do It!" (*Inc.* magazine, September 1991)

How Do You Get Relief?

The makers of Rolaids antacid conducted a nationwide survey on how Americans find relief. Almost 40% said they regularly play hooky and escape from work or school when feeling stressed. Of the same group, 23% stay home once a month because of stress.

Tea was cited over alcohol as the food or beverage that helps relieve stress the most. Women prefer tea more than men, who prefer beer or wine. Exercise, listening to music, and sleeping were the top remedies for relieving pressure. (*Fort Lauderdale News & Sun Sentinel*)

Seven Things Smart Parents Never Say

1. "You should have done it this way." When praise is mixed with criticism, kids tend to focus on the negative.
2. "Is that hair on your head or are you wearing a mop?" Teasing that comes from parents is the most painful teasing of all. It creates uncertainty in a child.
3. "You don't mean that." If you continually deny your child's feelings, they get the message that they shouldn't express them.
4. "That's the most beautiful picture I've ever seen." Kids who receive a steady stream of parental compliments are likely to experience a big letdown when they get into the world.

5. "Hey, you're a wildman." Kids believe what you tell them and will try to live up to it.
6. "Watch out- you're cruisin' for a bruisin'." Like false compliments, false threats undermine a parent's credibility.
7. "Not now." A persistent pattern of putting a child off can leave a lasting impact. (Harriet Webster, *Reader's Digest*, February 1996)

Attaboy!

In 1948, the president of Ford Motor Co. went to Germany to inspect its post-war production efforts. When he toured the Volkswagen plant, he said the little Beetle does not "meet the fundamental technical requirements of a motorcar." He came home from Germany and developed the Edsel.

Word Count

It's reported that talkative people speak about 12,000 sentences a day or about 100,000 words a day. Are you making your words count?

Missed Opportunity

Britain's greatest blunder in World War I happened in the Dardanelles, the strait of water in Turkey that connects the Aegean Sea to the Sea of Marmara and Constantinople.

Sir Winston Churchill recommended that the British, the greatest fleet in the world at the time, sail up the Dardanelles, take Constantinople, and end the war. On March 18, 1915, the invasion began. The first day went perfectly but at the end of the day, largely out of fear of the risk and danger ahead, the admirals decided against Churchill's recommendation. They decided to pull back and take a more cautious approach. Historians agree this missed opportunity allowed the war to go on for three more years.

Ten years after the aborted invasion, Admiral Roger Keys sailed up the narrows into Constantinople. When he arrived he said, "It would have been easier than I thought! We simply couldn't have failed! And because we didn't try, another million lives were lost."

They missed an opportunity because they were paralyzed with fear and afraid of risk.

General Failure

General George Custer had plans beyond Little Big Horn. He was out for the Presidency of the United States. Everything was going to fall into place: the fame he earned as the Union's youngest general in the Civil War had waned over the years, but he'd get back on top by clearing the Sioux tribes out of Yellowstone Country. As soon as Chief Sitting Bull was whipped, a rider would light out for the nearest telegraph office, sending word to St. Louis in time for the Democratic Party's convention. Custer would be swept into the 1876 Presidential nomination. As a military hero with a fresh victory, he'd trounce the Republicans as easily as he had conquered the Sioux.

Of course, you know what happened on Custer's road to the White House. He choked. More than ten thousand Sioux, Cheyenne and Crow, holding more than twenty thousand horses, were gathered for their Great Summer Conference. They had home-court advantage: they knew every ravine and ridge. Custer ignored the numbers his scouts brought in. His troops burned smoky campfires, tipping off their position to the enemy. Instead of verifying if his tactics were justified, Custer simply sent two hundred men into a direct and completely fatal charge.

Like Custer's last stand, failure is often a result of over-estimating your strength. (Pat Riley, *The Winner Within*)

"Make plans by seeking advice; if you wage war, obtain guidance." (Proverbs 20:18)

Are You an Optimist?

Positive thinking is more than blind faith. Optimistic people fare better than pessimists in almost every aspect of life. Optimists are also less susceptible to depression and physical ills.

Psychologists say that optimism and pessimism are habits we learn as children. Our parents are our role models. To become more positive, challenge negative thoughts that come your way, think like a winner, and set attainable goals toward things that give you hope.

I Can Do It, Really...

When the Port Authority of New York and New Jersey ran a help-wanted ad for electricians with expertise at using Sontag connectors, it got 170 responses – even though there is no such thing as a Sontag connector. The Authority ran the ad to find out how many applicants falsify resumes. (Peter LeVine in *Boardroom Reports*, July 15, 1993)

Growing into Greatness

A group of tourists were visiting a quaint little European village. An old man was sitting beside the road when a traveler asked, "Were any great men born in this village?"

The old man replied, "Nope, only babies."

The old timer's sarcastic answer is profound. There are no instant heroes or successes. Greatness takes time. It must grow and mature. (Leonard Ravenhill, *The Last Days Newsletter*)

It Can't Be Done

George Danzig was a senior Math major at Stanford University during the Depression. Because unemployment was so high, it was imperative that he score well on his final exam in order to have a slim chance at getting a teaching job. He stayed up all night studying for the exam and even arrived to class late. He settled in his desk and went through all of the problems on the test sheet. There were two more problems on the chalkboard. George worked and worked on the final two problems but he could not solve them.

To his surprise, George's professor told him that he could continue working on the two problems for a couple of days. George went home and spent hours and hours on the problems. He was able to answer one of them. But he could not answer the second one. He turned in his test knowing he had lost all chances of finding a job.

The next morning George was awakened by his professor pounding on his door. "George, George, you've made mathematics history!" the professor shouted. What George didn't know was that before the exam the professor explained to the class that those two problems were classic, unsolvable problems. Even Einstein could not solve them. Because George showed up late for the exam, he assumed that they were part of the test. He didn't know that the problems were unsolvable.

That very morning, George became the assistant to his professor and ended up teaching at Stanford for over 40 years.

It goes to show us what can be done when we choose not to be defeated. (Don Davidson in *Christian Single*, January 1994)

Ring Motivation

"When I was a kid in Louisville (KY) I had a job sacking groceries. I found a secondhand bicycle I just had to have. It was blue and beautiful. I didn't make much money at the grocery but I finally saved up enough to get that secondhand bicycle. I parked it behind the store, proud and happy. I worked hard for it. Then somebody stole it. Just about broke my heart. I walked all over Louisville that summer, looking for that bicycle. I walked and looked, looked and walked. Never found it to this day. But every time I got into the ring, I looked across at the other fighter and told myself, 'Hey, that's the guy that stole my bicycle!'" (Muhammad Ali)

Cobb's Confidence

In 1960, Hall of Fame baseball player Ty Cobb was asked how he thought he would bat against contemporary pitchers. Cobb's lifetime batting average was .367, but he said he probably wouldn't be able to top .300. "You've got to remember," he explained. "I'm 73."

Don't Worry, Be Happy (and Healthy)

People who score higher on standard stress tests are more likely to catch a cold when exposed to the virus. You are also a prime target for these pesky germs if you have a poor diet, don't exercise, smoke, don't get regular sleep, or drink alcohol. (*Today's Christian Woman*, January/February 1999)

Timely Thoughts

To remain youthful, remain useful.

The best place to spend your vacation is somewhere near your budget.

You will be happy in about the same degree that you are helpful.

You can't do anything by doing nothing.

Optimism

There are two rooms – one is full of brand new toys and the other is full of hay and horse manure. Two children are taken into the rooms. One is an optimist. The other child is a pessimist.

The pessimistic child looked in the first room and cried. "All of these wonderful toys and they will soon be broken!" Meanwhile, the optimistic child was in the second room shoveling and saying, "I know there's got to be a horse in here somewhere."

"It's just as easy to look for the good things in life as the bad."

Optimism (Part 2)

After Thomas Edison's 700th unsuccessful attempt to invent the electric light, he was asked by a *New York Times* reporter, "How does it feel to have failed 700 times?"

The great inventor responded, "I have not failed 700 times. I have not failed once. I have succeeded in proving that those 700 ways will not work. When I have eliminated the ways that will not work, I will find the way that will work."

Several thousand more of these successes followed, but Edison finally found the one that would work and invented the electric light. Failure is an attitude, not an outcome. (Harvey Mackay, *Beware the Naked Man Who Offers You His Shirt*)

"Past failures are guideposts for future success."

"Failure is merely an opportunity to start over again, wiser than before."

"Failure doesn't mean you'll never succeed – it will just take longer."

A List of Listening Skills

Listening is not just passive hearing. It is an active, participating experience in which you pay genuine attention to what the other person is saying. Here are some principles that should help you become a better listener:

1. Don't grab the conversation: "Yes, now take me, for instance..."
2. Don't let your gaze wander from the other person's face except momentarily.
3. Validate the feelings of the other: "Yes, I see what you mean."
4. Don't interrupt.
5. Don't try to top the other person's story or joke.
6. Ask appropriate questions: "What happened then?" or "How did you feel?"
7. Don't criticize.
8. Don't argue. (Cecil C. Osborne, *The Art of Getting Along with People*)

"Let the wise listen and add to their learning, and let the discerning get guidance..." (Proverbs 1:5)

"He who answers before listening – that is his folly and his shame." (Proverbs 18:13)

"My dear brothers, take note of this: Everyone should be quick to listen, slow to speak and slow to become angry..." (James 1:19)

Worth Considering

Babe Ruth hit 714 homeruns in his career. He struck out 1330 times.

Busyness

When not moving, a driver enjoys a field of vision of 180 degrees or more. At twenty miles per hour, the field of vision is reduced by approximately two-thirds. At forty miles per hour, the field of vision is further reduced by two-fifths. At sixty miles per hour, the field of vision is barely wider than the width of the beams of the headlights.

This illustrates the principle that the faster the pace of life, the less perspective one can achieve.

Happily Ever After

A little girl had just heard the story *Snow White* for the first time. So full of enthusiasm that she could hardly contain herself, she retold the fairy tale to her mother. After telling about how Prince Charming had arrived on his beautiful white horse and kissed Snow White back to life, she asked her mother, "And do you know what happened then?"

"Yes," replied her mom, "they lived happily ever after."

"No," responded Suzie, with a frown, "they got married."

With childlike innocence, Suzie had spoken a partial truth without realizing it. Getting married and living happily ever after are not necessarily synonymous.

"If a man has enough horse sense to treat his wife like a thoroughbred, she'll never turn into an old nag."

"Marriage is not finding the person with whom you can live, but finding the person with whom you can't live without." (Howard Hendricks)

Timely Thoughts

"Don't pray for rain if you're going to complain about the mud."

"It pays to advertise. There are 26 mountains in Colorado higher than Pike's Peak."

"A foot is a device for finding furniture in the dark."

Organize Your Day

Divide your day into blocks of time, then work in one uninterrupted block at a time. Take breaks between blocks. Also: Know what is most important for you to accomplish. Focus on those tasks that bring you closer to your goals so you do not waste time.

Five Mistakes to Avoid

1) Anxiety over today's trials.
2) Worry over tomorrow's problems.
3) Criticism of a friend's infirmities.
4) Unbelief in God's promises.
5) Pride over your accomplishments.

Decisions, Decisions

Whenever you're called on to make up your mind,
And you're hampered by not having any,
The simplest way to solve the dilemma you'll find,
Is simply by flipping a penny.
No, not so that chance shall decide the affair,
As you're passively standing there moping.
But as soon as the penny is up in the air,
You'll suddenly know what you're hoping. (Piet Hein)

"A wise man changes his mind, a fool – never."

"An executive is a person who can take as long as he wants to make a snap decision."

Timely Trivia

The Associated Press conducted a survey recently among the inner-city kids of America. They asked whom they most admired. Michael Jordan tied for the lead with God.

Drunk drivers cause 39% of all fatal car accidents. They can drive an average of between 200 and 2000 times before getting caught. (*Bottom Line*, 12/15/98)

Marriage Quotes

"Only two things are necessary to keep one's wife happy. One is to let her think she is having her own way, and the other, to let her have it." (Lyndon B. Johnson)

"Love is blind, but marriage restores one's sight." (G. C. Lichtenberg)

"Marriage halves our griefs, doubles our joys, and quadruples our expenses." (Anonymous)

Observe the mother and take the daughter. (Turkish proverb)

Always a Critic

An old man had a grandson who rode a donkey while they were traveling from one city to another. The man heard some people say, "Look at that old man suffering on his feet while that strong young boy is totally capable of walking."

Then the old man rode the donkey while the boy walked. And he heard some people say, "Look at that, a healthy man making the poor young boy suffer. Can you believe that?"

So the man and the boy rode the donkey. Then they heard people say, "Look at those heavy brutes making that poor donkey suffer." They got off and walked, until they heard someone say, "Look at that waste – a perfectly good donkey not being used."

Finally, the boy is seen walking and the man carrying the donkey. No matter what you do, someone will always criticize it.

"A critic is a legless man who teaches running."

"To avoid criticism, say nothing, do nothing, and be nothing."

"There are two things that are bad for the heart: running upstairs and running down people."

"Don't use a hatchet to remove a fly from your friend's forehead."

Facts & Figures

Have you ever wondered about the religious preferences of Americans? Protestant 62%, Roman Catholic 20%, No religion 7%, Non-Christian 4%, Jewish 3%. (*Newsweek*)

According to *USA Today*, people who attend church regularly live 10% longer than those who do not. The life expectancy of those who attend church weekly is 82. Non-church goers live an average of 75 years.

Weaving Habits

Habits are like a cable. Each day we do something in a pattern. We intertwine one thread with another. As the threads are woven together, a cable is formed. On any particular day, the thread we added was too small to be noticed. But, after many threads have been woven in, we find that together they have become a practically unbreakable cable.

So it is with habits. Daily practices over time become habits that are practically unbreakable --so be careful what you weave.

"Habits are first cobwebs, then cables."

"The nature of men is always the same; it is their habits that separate them." (Confucius)

"'Tis easier to prevent bad habits than to break them."

"One of the advantages of being disorderly is that one is constantly making exciting discoveries." (A. A. Milne)

Timely Trivia

Mark Twain didn't even make it through elementary school.

It takes six months to build a Rolls Royce... and thirteen hours to build a Toyota.

Math Whiz?

Archimedes, one of the greatest of the ancient Greek mathematicians and scientists, was working on a math problem when his native city of Syracuse was conquered by the Roman general Marcellus in 212 B.C. The scientist ignored the final assault and continued working on his math while the enemy entered the gates of the city. As the Roman soldiers came down the street where Archimedes was, he continued to work the problem in the sand and offered no resistance, even as one of them ran him through with a sword and killed him.

Many people are like Archimedes, oblivious to what is really happening around them until it is too late to do anything about it.

Fleeting Fame

A reporter once asked Walt Disney how it felt to be a celebrity. "It feels fine," he replied, "when being a celebrity helps me get a choice seat for a football game. As far as I can remember, being a celebrity has never helped me make a good picture, or a good shot in a polo game, or command the obedience of my daughter, or impress my wife. It doesn't even seem to help keep fleas off our dogs and, if being a celebrity won't give me an advantage over a couple of fleas, then I guess there can't be that much in being a celebrity after all."

"Fame usually comes to those who are thinking about something else." (Oliver Wendell Holmes, Jr.)

Possibility Thinking

"If you think you are beaten, you are.
If you think you dare not, you don't.
If you like to win, but you think you can't, it's almost certain you won't.

"If you think you'll lose, you're lost,
For out in the world we find,
Success begins with a fellow's will –
It's all in the state of mind.
"If you think you are outclassed, you are. You've got to think high to rise.
You've got to be sure of yourself before
You can ever win a prize.

"Life's battles don't always go
To the stronger or faster man,
But soon or late the man who wins
Is the man who thinks he can." (Napoleon Hill)

Procrastination

While cleaning out his desk, a man found a shoe repair ticket that was ten years old. Figuring that he had nothing to lose, he went to the shop and gave the ticket to the repairman, who began to search the back room for the unclaimed shoes. After several minutes, he reappeared and gave the ticket back to the customer.

"What's wrong?" asked the man. "Couldn't you find my shoes?"

"Oh, I found them," replied the repairman, " and they'll be ready next Friday."

"Procrastination is the assassination of motivation."

Timely Quotes

"The most important trip you may take in life is meeting people halfway."

"Even more exasperating than the guy who thinks he knows it all is the one who really does."

"Treat a person as he is, and he will remain as he is. Treat him as he could be, and he will become what he should be."

"History, although sometimes made up of the few acts of the great, is more often shaped by the many acts of the small."

Encouraging Words

Bear Bryant, legendary football coach at the University of Alabama, was once asked to explain his philosophy of coaching:

"There's just three things I ever say to my players: 'If anything goes bad, then I did it. If anything goes semi-good, then we did it. If anything goes real good, then you did it.' That's all it takes to get people to win football games for you. I can do that better than anybody."

"Encouragement is like a peanut butter sandwich – the more you spread it around, the better things stick together."

When he was a young boy the great painter Benjamin West decided to paint a picture of his sister while his mother was not at home. He got out bottles of ink and started, but soon had an awful mess. His mother eventually returned and of course saw the mess. Instead of scolding him, she picked up the portrait and declared, "What a beautiful picture of your sister!" Then she kissed him. Later in life West said, "With that kiss I became a painter."

Principles for Success

John Wooden, one of the greatest college basketball coaches of all time, cites eight principles for success:

1. Fear no opponent. Respect every opponent.
2. Remember, it's the perfection of the smallest details that make big things happen.
3. Keep in mind that hustle makes up for many a mistake.
4. Be more interested in character than reputation.
5. Be quick, but do not hurry.
6. Understand that the harder you work, the more luck you will have.
7. Know that valid self-analysis is crucial for improvement.
8. Remember that there is no substitute for hard work and careful planning. Failing to prepare is preparing to fail. (*FYI: Georgia Views and News*)

Take This To The Office

- Communication is the secret to success...pass it on.
- The best way to predict the future is to create it.
- It takes months to find a customer...seconds to lose one.
- Attitude is a little thing that makes a big difference.
- Service is the lifeblood of any organization. Everything flows from it and is nourished by it. Customer service is not a department...it's an attitude.
- Success is a journey not a destination.
- Countless, unseen details are often the only difference between mediocre and magnificent.
- Unless you try something beyond what you have already mastered, you will never grow.

Who Am I?

I am your constant companion,
I am your greatest helper or your heaviest burden.
I will push you onward or drag you down to failure.
I am at your command.

Half of the tasks that you do you might just as well turn over to me and I will do them quickly and correctly.

I am easily managed,
you must merely be firm with me.
Show me exactly how you want something done;
after a few lessons I will do it automatically.
I am the servant of all great people and alas of all failures as well.

Those who are great I have made great, those who are failures I have made failures.
I am not a machine, but I work with all the precision of a machine, plus the intelligence of a person.
Now you may run me for profit or you may run me for ruin.
It makes no difference to me.
Take me, train me, be firm with me, and I will lay the world at your feet.
Be easy with me and I will destroy you.

Who am I?

I am called Habit. (Dave Ramsey, *Financial Peace*)

Timely Thought

"Be concerned with ideals, not just deals."

Practice Makes Perfect

Grover Cleveland Alexander, one of the greatest pitchers to play baseball, grew up on a farm. Like many young boys, he dreamed of becoming a professional baseball player. Between chores on the farm, he'd throw apples, stones – anything to sharpen his skills.

He bought a few balls, nailed an old mitt to the chicken coop, and he would throw at it for hours. Soon he could hit the mitt nine times out of ten.

Later, when he became famous, reporters raved over his skill and "natural" ability. But no one knew anything about the drudgery of throwing at the old mitt on the chicken coop.

Greatness doesn't always come naturally. Usually it has to be developed with practice and persistence.

"Things work out best for those who make the best of the way things work out."

"Great dancers are not great because of their technique. They are great because of their passion." (Martha Graham)

One Final Note

Here's interesting advice: Write a last love letter and file it with your will. In it, say and re-say all the things you have felt for your spouse over the years. Update the letter whenever you wish. This helps overcome the guilt that a spouse often feels over things left unsaid. (Carol Krueger, *222 Terrific Tips for Two*)

Overheard

"Beware of the barrenness of a busy life."

"Opportunities are seldom labeled."

The Naked Truth

Have you ever wondered why we use the expression, "The Naked Truth?"

According to an old fable, Truth and Falsehood went swimming together and Falsehood stole Truth's clothing. Truth went naked rather than dress in Falsehood's garments.

Train your mind to think on what is true and right. Trash that which is false and wrong. Your habit of truthfulness can be your greatest contribution to this generation.

When Petrarch, an Italian poet, was summoned to appear in court, the judge closed the book saying, "As to you, Petrarch, your word is sufficient." (*Seeds From the Sower*, Vol. 20, No. 4)

Be Persistent

The original business plan for Federal Express was given a failing grade on the college exam of the company's founder, Fred Smith. Colonel Sanders went to more than 1000 places trying to sell his recipe for fried chicken before he found an interested buyer. (Jim Donovan, *Handbook to a Happier Life*)

When my ship finally comes in, I'll probably be at the airport.

Five Votes of Confidence

Today is a new day. Therefore,
1) I refuse to be shackled by yesterday's failures.
2) What I don't know will no longer be an intimidation – it will be an opportunity.
3) I will not allow people to define my mood, method, image, or mission.
4) I will pursue a mission greater than myself by making at least one person happy they saw me.
5) I will have no time for self-pity, gossip, or negativism... from myself or from others. (Max Lucado)

A Short Course in Human Relations

The six most important words: "I admit I made a mistake."
The five most important words: "You did a good job."
The four most important words: "What is your opinion?"
The three most important words: "If you please."
The two most important words: "Thank you."
The one most important word: "We"
The least important word: "I"
(*Bits and Pieces*)

Optimist Creed

In his *Creed for Optimists*, Christian D. Larsen tells you how you can be *somebody*.
- Be so strong that nothing can disturb your peace of mind.
- Talk health, happiness, and prosperity to every person you meet.
- Make all your friends feel there is something special in them.
- Look at the sunny side of everything.
- Think only of the best, work only for the best, and expect only the best.
- Be as enthusiastic about the success of others as you are about your own.
- Forget the mistakes of the past and press on to the greater achievements of the future.
- Give everyone a smile.

- Spend so much time improving yourself that you have no time left to criticize others.
- Be too big for worry and too noble for anger.

"For every criticism you make of someone's job performance, make sure you give four compliments."

Who is Happy?

A survey asked, "Who are the happiest people?" These were the four winning answers:

1. A craftsman or artist whistling over a job well done.
2. A child building sand castles.
3. A mother bathing her baby.
4. A doctor who has finished a difficult operation and saved a life.

Note that money, power, and possessions play no part in any of the answers. (*FYI: Georgia Views and News*, June 1998)

Twist of Fate

In the early 1960's, Reynolds Guyer worked at his family's sales-promotion company designing packages and displays. He also created premiums – the gifts people get for sending in boxtops and proofs-of-purchase.

One day in 1965, the 29 year-old Guyer and his crew started work on a premium for a shoe polish company. "One idea," he says, "was to have kids standing on this mat with squares that told them where to put their feet...but I thought, this is bigger than just a premium."

He expanded the mat to 4' x 6' and turned it into a game. "I got the secretaries and the designers and everyone together to play. You know, in 1965 no one ever touched. It really broke all the rules of propriety having people stand so close together."

At first it was a flop. No one knew what to make of a game where people were the main playing pieces. But when Johnny Carson and Eva Gabor played it on the "Tonight Show" in 1966, America got the point. Overnight, Twister became a runaway hit.

Timely Time Tips

Don't waste time regretting your failures.

Don't waste time feeling guilty about what you don't do.

Try to enjoy whatever you are doing.

Do first things first.

Work smarter not harder.

Concentrate on one thing at a time.

Don't waste other people's time.

Handle each piece of paper only once.

Continually ask, "What's the best use of my time right now?" (Alan Lakein, *How to Get Control of Your Time and Your Life*)

Quotable

"Doubt is often the beginning of wisdom." (M. Scott Peck)

The Value of Friendship

During World War II, the enemy conducted experiments to find the most effective type of punishment for extracting information from prisoners. They found that solitary confinement was the most effective. After a few days of solitary confinement, most men would tell all.

That's why we need friends – without friends and fellowship we too become easy prey for temptation and abandonment of our values.

Timely Trivia

According to a national survey, the automobile is America's most important invention. 34% of Americans chose the car. 28% chose the light bulb. 17% selected the telephone. The personal computer and aspirin tied for fourth. (Does it surprise you that computers and aspirin go together?) (*The Executive Speechwriter Newsletter*, Vol. 13, No. 4)

On any given day, 20% of Americans are dieting.

The average American throws out 1905 pounds of garbage each year.

Seasoned Character

A couple came to the police department wanting to dispose of some ammunition. They handed the desk officer a wooden box and explained that it contained two bullets an uncle had given them as souvenirs from World War II.

"We didn't know what to do with them," the woman explained. "So all these years, we've kept the bullets in the bottom drawer of our china cabinet, away from our children."

The officer assured the couple he'd dispose of the bullets safely. But when he took one out of the box the top came off, revealing a strange black substance. His suspicions aroused, the officer removed the top of the other bullet and found a hard white substance. There was no doubt about it. The bullets were souvenir salt and pepper shakers.

Like the bullets, our true character is found on the inside. We may appear as a certain kind of person on the outside but character reveals who we are on the inside. Character is not who people think we are but who we know we are.

Timely Quotes

"The word *no* carries a lot more meaning when spoken by a parent who also knows how to say *yes*." (Joyce Maynard, *Parenting*)

"There are two ways of spreading light: to be the candle or the mirror that reflects it." (Edith Wharton)

"The value of marriage is not that adults produce children, but that children produce adults." (Peter De Vries, *The Tunnel of Love*)

"Nobody gets to live life backward. Look ahead – that's where your future lies." (Ann Landers)

"'Tis an ill cook that cannot lick his own fingers." (William Shakespeare)

About Time

Time magazine noted that back in the 1960's, expert testimony was given to a subcommittee of the Senate on time management. The essence of it was that because of advances in technology, within twenty years or so people would have to radically cut back on how many hours a week they worked, or how many weeks a year they worked, or else they would have to start retiring sooner. The great challenge, they said, was what people would do with all their free time. (John Ortberg, *The Life You've Always Wanted*)

Timely Tip

Take Vitamin C. It works in your body as a scavenger, picking up all sorts of trash, including viruses. Vitamin C can shorten the length of a cold from 7 days to 2 days. It has been proven to lower cholesterol and decrease arthritis pain, as well as many other benefits. (Mary Hunt, *Tiptionary*)

Success Thoughts

The next time things aren't going right, you might regain some confidence by remembering that:
   1) The best basketball players make only about 50 percent of their shots.
   2) The successful actor is turned down 29 out of 30 times when auditioning for roles in TV commercials. (Denis Waitley, *The Joy of Working*)

"Be strong and very courageous; be careful to do according to all the law which Moses my servant commanded you; do not turn from it to the right or to the left, so that you may have success wherever you go." (Joshua 1:7)

Success is having:
   - lived well
   - laughed often
   - loved much
   - labored diligently

Timely Thought

"Time is life – nothing more, nothing less. The way you spend your hours and your days is the way you spend your life." (John Boykin)

Optimistic Quotes

"It's just as easy to look for the good things in life as the bad."

"The worst pest in the world is a pessimist."

"In the long run the pessimist may be proven right, but the optimist has a better time on the trip."

Perseverance Pays

Many great men and women of history were not afraid to fail. Choose any field of life and you will find a successful person who persevered until they accomplished their task.

Politics: Abraham Lincoln failed in eight straight elections before he finally won the presidency.

Business: Walt Disney and Henry Ford both declared personal bankruptcy prior to their journey to the top of their fields.

Sports: Babe Ruth not only held baseball's homerun record. He also held the strikeout record too!

Writing: The best seller *Jonathan Livingston Seagull* by Richard Bach, was rejected by dozens of publishers before it finally found a home.

Entertainment: Search the life of any major star and you'll find at some point they had to pump gas, drive a cab, or wait tables until their big break came along.

Public Speaking: Perhaps America's greatest public speaker, Zig Ziglar, gave 3000 free speeches before he ever got paid for one.

Success Secret

"Sir, what is the secret of your success?" a reporter asked a bank president.

"Two words."

"And what are they?"

"Right decisions."

"And how do you make the right decisions?" replied the reporter.

"One word."

"What is that word?"

"Experience," responded the president.

"How do you get experience?"

"Two words."

"What are they?" asked the reporter.

"Wrong decisions."

"The only place you find success before work is in the dictionary." (May Smith)

"The secret of getting ahead is getting started. The secret of getting started is breaking your complex overwhelming tasks into small manageable tasks, and then starting on the first one." (Mark Twain)

"Ideas are a dime a dozen. People who put them into action are priceless."

"Whoever wants to become great among you must become your servant, and whoever wants to be first must be slave of all." (Mark 10:43)

Timely Thoughts
(From *Poor Richard's Almanac* by Benjamin Franklin)

"Tomorrow, every fault is amended; but that tomorrow never comes."

"Neglect mending a small fault, and it will soon be a great one."

"If you have time, don't wait for time."

"An egg today is better than a hen tomorrow."

"Do you love life? Then do not squander time, for that's the stuff life is made of."

"You may delay, but time will not."

Teamwork

Teamwork is the ability to work together toward a common vision. The ability to direct individual accomplishment toward organizational objectives. It is the fuel that allows common people to attain uncommon results.

Scars into Stars

A young man dreamed of working in his father's business. He saw himself in a plush office with a pretty secretary. But his father said, "You'll start at the bottom. Your job will be to water the hundreds of plants in our building."

The son was humbled, but he turned his disappointment into delight. He came to work with his business card that read, "Plant Manager."

You can't always control your circumstances, but you can be in charge of your attitude.

Viktor Frankl, an author and psychiatrist, was a prisoner in World War II concentration camps. His father, mother, brother, and wife were killed in the cruel camps. In his book, *Man's Search for Meaning*, Frankl wrote, "Everything can be taken from a man but one thing: the last of the human freedoms – to choose one's attitude in any given set of circumstances, to choose one's own way."

Refuse to be destroyed by disappointments. Learn to turn scars into stars.

When It Pays to Look Bad

A Minneapolis businessman was on vacation in Waikiki over Christmas. He went to the beach for hours every day and acquired an immaculate tan – from the neck down. Not a ray of sunshine reached his face, which he kept totally shaded by a hat, sunrise to sunset. His friends were curious, of course, but too embarrassed to ask him why, figuring that he might have medical problems that kept him from exposing his face to the sun. Finally an acquaintance asked him. The businessman laughed and said, "Who, me? A skin problem? Nope. Next week I have to testify before the state legislature and I'm asking them for a huge subsidy, and I wouldn't dare be caught with a tan on my face."

Moral: It usually pays to look good, but sometimes it pays a lot more to look bad. (Harvey McKay, *Swim With The Sharks Without Being Eaten Alive*)

Quotes on Success

- You can't climb the ladder of success with your hands in your pockets.
- To be a success, sometimes a person must have enough courage to make a fool of himself.
- It is better to try to do something and fail than to do nothing and succeed.
- Some men succeed because they are destined to, but most men succeed because they are determined to.
- A person is successful when he has learned to live well, laugh often, and love truly.
- A successful man is usually an average man who had a chance or took a chance.

Colors

Here are some things researchers have discovered about people and color:

PINK – Studies show that people almost always believe pastries from a pink box taste better than from any other color box.

People are willing to pay more for personal services (e.g., haircuts) performed by people wearing pink.

Men believe pink products do the best job, but don't want to be seen buying them. If they think someone is watching, they'll choose something brown or blue.

ORANGE – When it's used on a product, it loudly proclaims that the product is for everyone.

PALE BLUE – Pale blue can actually make people feel cooler. Designers often use it in places where men work, because men feel five degrees warmer than a woman in the same room temperature.

Blue inhibits the desire to eat. In fact, researchers say people tend to eat less from blue plates.

Since blue is associated with eating less, marketers use it to sell products like club soda, skim milk, and cottage cheese.

GREEN – Not used to sell meat. It reminds people of mold.

Is That Understood?

Some of us are like Christopher Columbus when it comes to our understanding:

He didn't know where he was going.
He didn't know where he was when he got there.
He didn't know where he had been when he returned.

Reputation Reflections

We may be known by the following:

1. What we want most
2. What we think about most
3. How we use our money
4. What we do with our leisure time
5. The company we enjoy
6. Who and what we admire
7. What we laugh at (A. W. Tozer)

"No one raises his reputation by lowering others."

"Reputation is what you need to get a job; character is what you need to keep one."

For Parents of Teens

"They now seem to love luxury, they have bad manners and contempt for authority, they show disrespect for adults and spend their time hanging around places gossiping with one another. They are ready to contradict their parents, monopolize the conversation and company, eat gluttonously, and tyrannize their teachers."

Some things never change. Socrates wrote the statement above over 2000 years ago. The conflict between teenagers and parents is an old, yet natural, problem.

McAdon't

Bob McAdoo was the NBA's Rookie of the Year in 1973 and Most Valuable Player in 1975. For three seasons he averaged over 32 points per game. He developed the nickname "Doo" because of his ability to make things happen.

Unfortunately, his teams did not fare well. He took all of the responsibility since he was the prize player. Because he tried to do it all on his own, he became a very selfish player. In his fifth year, he began to be traded from team to team frequently - six times in six years. Each time he was traded for less and less money. Over time, Bob McAdoo's nickname changed from "Doo" to "McAdon't." (Pat Riley, *The Winner Within*)

The Lazy Farmer

A farmer was sitting on his porch when a stranger came by and asked, "How's it going?"

"Tolerable," replied the farmer. "Two weeks ago a tornado came along and knocked down all the trees I would have had to chop down for this winter's firewood. Then last week lightning struck the brush I had planned to burn to clear the fields for planting."

"That's remarkable," the stranger responded, "What are you doing now?"

The farmer answered, "Waiting for an earthquake to come along and shake the taters out of the ground."

"If you don't want to work
You have to work
To earn enough money
So that you won't have to work."
(Ogden Nash)

Five Mistakes of Man

Cicero, the Roman statesman and philosopher, wrote the following some 2000 years ago.

Five Mistakes of Man:
1. The delusion that personal gain is made by crushing others.

2. The tendency to worry about things that cannot be changed or corrected.

3. Insisting that a thing is impossible because we cannot accomplish it.

4. Refusing to set aside trivial preferences.

5. Neglecting development and refinement of the mind, and not acquiring the habit of reading and studying. (*Bits & Pieces*)

Timely Thoughts

"Never mistake knowledge for wisdom. One helps you make a living; the other helps you make a life." (Sandra Carey)

"Character is what you know you are, not what others think you are." (Marva Collins & Civia Tamarkin)

"Be an optimist – at least until they start moving animals in pairs to Cape Kennedy." (Current Comedy)

"Death and taxes may always be with us, but at least death doesn't get any worse." (Los Angeles Times Syndicate)

"All of us could take a lesson from the weather. It pays no attention to criticism." (North Dekalb Kiwanis Club Beacon)

"Any time you think you have influence, try ordering around someone else's dog." (The Cockle Bur)

"It's not easy taking my problems one at a time when they refuse to get in line." (Ashleigh Brilliant)

"Don't just pretend that you love others. Really love them. Hate what is wrong. Stand on the side of the good. Love each other with genuine affection, and take delight in honoring each other. (Romans 12:9-10)

Be Nice

Five Etiquette Mistakes Even Polite People Make:

1. Saying your phone number too quickly on someone's voice mail or answering machine.
2. Finishing someone else's sentence...idea...or story.
3. Artlessly ending a business lunch or dinner. Instead of looking at your watch, excuse yourself to the restroom. On your way, ask the waiter to bring you the check after you return to the table.
4. Rushing through office doors or around corridors – always bad form.
5. Not writing a thank you note. (Nancy Tuckerman, former White House staff coordinator to Jacqueline Kennedy)

Everybody's a Critic

Adventuresome and courageous pioneers have often faced the critical laughter of jealous observers.

The first American steamboat took thirty-two hours to go from New York to Albany. People laughed.

The horse and buggy passed the early motor car as if it were standing still (it usually was). People laughed.

The first electric light bulb was so dim that people had to use a gas lamp to see it. They laughed.

The first airplane came down fifty-nine seconds after it left the ground. People laughed.

If you try to tackle a big job, or if you have new ideas, expect criticism!

Timely Advice

My basic principle is that you don't make decisions because they are easy; you don't make them because they are cheap; you don't make them because they are popular; you make them because they are right. (Theodore Hesburgh, former president of the University of Notre Dame)

"Success is 99 percent failure." (Soichiro Honda, Founder, Honda Motor Corporation)

"Good enough never is." (Debbi Field, Founder, Mrs. Field's Cookies)

"Shoot for the moon, even if you miss, you'll be among the stars."

"Watch your thoughts; they become words. Watch your words; they become actions. Watch your actions; they become habits. Watch your habits; they become character. Watch your character; it becomes your destiny."

"Lots of people want to ride with you in the limo, but what you want is someone who will take the bus with you when the limo breaks down." (Oprah Winfrey)

"Angels can fly because they take themselves lightly."

"Never be afraid to try something new. Remember, amateurs built the ark; professionals built the Titanic."

Marriage Secret

Lasting marriages owe less to true love, great sex, or even a sense of commitment than to an intimate friendship between husband and wife. In a survey, 351 couples married 15 years or longer were asked how their marriages survived in an increasingly turbulent world. Most respondents credited a positive attitude toward their spouses, as characterized by such statements as "My spouse is my best friend," and "I like my spouse as a person."

Though such sentiments sound trite, they truly spell the difference between a union that lasts and one that ends in divorce. (Robert Lauer, Ph.D.)

Pulling For You

A stranger was driving in the country and his car skidded into a ditch. He found a farmer who had a mule named Dusty, and the farmer offered to help.

He hitched Dusty to the car and yelled, "Pull Charlie, pull Sammy," but the mule didn't move. Then he yelled, "Pull Dusty!" and the mule jerked the car out of the ditch.

"Why," asked the stranger, "did you call your mule by three different names?"

"Dusty's blind," the farmer said. "If he thought he had to do it alone, he wouldn't even try."

You are not alone. Look around today and take note of all the friends, coworkers and family members who are pulling for you and with you.

When you're helping others, you help yourself.

Four Deadly Words

The old saying is that "If it ain't broke, don't fix it." The people who make it big are the ones who fix it before it's broke. They force the competition to play catch up. They make their own rules, and the others have to play by them.

The four deadly words for any organization are "It can't be done." Several examples from the past prove that this is not a good attitude to take.

One of them is Harry Warner. He was president of Warner Brothers Movie Studios in 1927 when talking pictures were just coming on to the silver screen. Mr. Warner's comment on this technological breakthrough was: "Who wants to hear actors talk?"

Then there's Robert Millikan, Nobel Prize winner in physics in 1923. He said, "There is no likelihood man can ever tap the power of the atom."

Charles Duell, head of the U.S. Patent Office in 1899 said, "Everything that can be invented, has been invented."

What did these men have in common? They were completely wrong. Success comes when a person is willing to do something different by taking risks, defying the odds, and even looking foolish. (Harvey Mackay, *Swim with the Sharks without Being Eaten Alive*)

Book List

A few books that will change your life:

Tyranny of the Urgent, Charles E. Hummel

Simplify Your Life and *Living the Simple Life*, Elaine St. James

Your Money or Your Life, Joe Dominguez and Vicki Robin

Financial Peace, Dave Ramsey

Freedom of Simplicity, Richard J. Foster

Ordering Your Private World, Gordon MacDonald

Honest to God, Bill Hybels

The Bible

"God's word is a lamp to my feet, and a light to my path."
(Psalm 119:105)

Crisis? What Crisis?

Jim Lovell, Commander of the near fatal Apollo 13 mission, was once asked how his experience on Apollo 13 has changed him. His response: "Crises don't bother me anymore."

Daily Balance

What would you do if your bank credited your account every morning with $84,600, but every night canceled whatever you failed to use during the day?

You'd draw out every cent of the account, wouldn't you?

You have such a bank. Every morning God credits your account with 84,600 seconds. Every night He cancels whatever you failed to use.

You can't buy time and you can't save it. You can only spend it. If you don't spend it well, you waste it.

Yesterday is a canceled check. Tomorrow is a promissory note. Today is all the cash you have. Spend it wisely. (*Seeds From The Sower*)

"Let us draw near to God with a sincere heart in full assurance of faith." (Hebrews 10:22)

Time Poor

While American society is rich in goods, it is extremely time poor. Many societies in third world nations, by contrast, are poor in material possessions, by our standards, but they are rich in time. They are not driven or hurried. They live with a sense that there is adequate time to do what needs to be done each day. (Robert Banks)

Quotables

"Opportunities are usually disguised as hard work, so most people don't recognize them." (Ann Landers)

"Knowing is not enough; we must apply. Willing is not enough; we must do." (Goethe)

"Experience is knowing a lot of things you shouldn't do." (William S. Knudsen)

"The successful person is the individual who forms the habit of doing what the failing person doesn't like to do." (Donald Riggs)

"Hurry is not of the devil, hurry is the devil." (Carl Jung)

"The way I see it, if you want the rainbow, you gotta put up with the rain." (Dolly Parton)

A Matter of Perspective

A wise old farmer was approached by a stranger one day and asked how much he thought his prize Jersey cow was worth. The farmer thought for a moment, looked the stranger over, then asked, "Are you the tax assessor or has she just been killed by your car?"

Life Lessons

Two construction workers sat down at noon to eat. One opened his lunch box and screamed, "Baloney! I hate baloney! Everyday this week I've had baloney sandwiches!"

His friend tried to settle him down. "Take it easy. Why don't you just tell your wife that you are tired of baloney and ask her to fix something else for a change?"

"Wife?" the worker replied. "I make my own lunches."

The fact is...most of the baloney in our lives, we put there ourselves.

"If you want life's best, see to it that life gets your best."

"More important than the length of life is how we spend each day."

"Life is a canvas. You fill in the picture."

"Life is either what you make of it, or what it makes of you."

"Half of our troubles are due to the fact that we live on the assumption that this is the only life and only world."

"Your life is like a coin. You can spend it any way you wish, but you can spend it only once."
"The most important things in life are not things."

The Power of Knowledge

An expert was called in to fix a broken factory machine. With the superintendent looking on, the expert assessed the situation, spotted the problem, took out a hammer and tapped the machine twice in the same spot. The machine started right up. He informed the superintendent that his bill would be $250. The superintendent was furious. "Two hundred and fifty dollars!" he shouted, "All you did was tap it with a hammer. I want an itemized statement of the charges on my desk by tomorrow morning!"

The next day when the superintendent arrived for work, he found the following bill on his desk:

Tapping with a hammer: $1
Knowing where to tap: <u>$249</u>
Total $250

(Robert Allen, *Achieving Financial Liberty*)

Famous Errors

Here's a reminder that even the best of us mess up at times. These baseball Hall of Fame members hold some records that they'd rather forget. For example:

Babe Ruth held the record for the most career strikeouts until it was broken by another Hall of Fame member, Reggie Jackson.

Hank Aaron hit into more double plays than any other player in history.

In 1915, Ty Cobb set a season record for number of times thrown out while attempting to steal a base.

Walter Johnson, one of the greatest pitchers of all time, holds the record for hitting the most batters.

Roberto Clemente holds the All-Star game record for most consecutive strikeouts.

"We have this treasure in jars of clay to show that this all-surpassing power is from God and not from us" (2 Corinthians 4:7)

Timely Quotes

(The following were taken from the book, *The Winner Within*, by former Los Angeles Lakers coach Pat Riley)

"I have always thought the actions of men the best interpreters of their thoughts." (John Locke)

"To appreciate heaven well, 'tis good for a man to have some fifteen minutes in hell." (Will Carleton)

"The world is full of willing people, some willing to work, the others willing to let them." (Robert Frost)

"Some of us are like wheelbarrows – only useful when pushed, and very easily upset." (Jack Herbert)

"If you can dream it, you can do it. Always remember that this whole thing was started by a mouse." (Walt Disney)

More From Poor Richard
(Quotes from *Poor Richard's Almanac* by Benjamin Franklin)

"Content makes poor men rich.   Discontent makes rich men poor."

"Old boys have their playthings as well as young ones. The difference is only in the price."

"He that is rich need not live sparingly and he that can live sparingly need not be rich."

"Beware of little expenses. A small leak will sink a great ship."

"A man between two lawyers is like a fish between two cats."

"Be civil to all; serviceable to many; familiar with few; friend to one; enemy to none."

Quotable

"You're not a failure if you fall down, but you are if you stay down."

"Oversleeping is a poor way to make your dreams come true."
"Forbidden fruit is responsible for many a bad jam."

"Preachers make us happy. Some when they start preaching and others when they stop."

In my parent's generation, parents had a lot of kids. Now kids have a lot of parents.

"Washington's face has been on our money for a long time. Now Washington's hands are on it too."

"Success comes in cans, not in cannots."

"Some people make good livings, but poor lives."

A New Start

Ben Franklin was called a poor mathematician and George Bernard Shaw was considered a bad speller. Albert Einstein, Salvador Dali, and Edgar Allen Poe were expelled from school. Thomas Edison was at the bottom of his class. Abraham Lincoln was criticized as "showing no promise."

Have you failed? Start over. Remember that winners never quit. They just have the courage to get back up after they fall.

Mrs. Hawthorne's Trust

Heartbroken Nathaniel went home to tell his wife he had been fired from his job. Sophia surprised him with an exclamation of joy. "Now you can write your book!"

"Yes," replied the man, with sagging confidence, "and what shall we live on while I am writing it?"

To his amazement, she opened a drawer and pulled out a substantial amount of money. "Where on earth did you get that?" he exclaimed.

"I've always known you were a man of genius," she told him. "I knew that someday you would write a masterpiece. So every week, out of the money you gave me for housekeeping, I saved a little bit. Here is enough to last us for one whole year."

From her confidence came one of the greatest novels of American literature, *The Scarlet Letter* by Nathaniel Hawthorne. (David Jeremiah, *The Power of Encouragement*)

Silly Mistake

What do you get when you mix silicone oil with boric acid? Why, Silly Putty, of course! James Wright, a General Electric scientist did just that in 1943 when he was working to find a way to make synthetic rubber for the war effort. This stuff was one of many failures in the process. He was preparing to throw it away when a co-worker noticed that the substance had the peculiar characteristics of being able to stretch like taffy, yet break into pieces if hit with a hammer. It could also bounce higher than a rubber ball. Mr. Wright took some home and used it as a conversation piece until 1950 when a businessman convinced him to sell it as a toy.

Fifty years later, 4500 tons of Silly Putty has been sold. That's enough to make a wad the size of the Goodyear blimp!

Who would have thought that a goofy chemical mistake would wind up being one of the most popular and enduring toys of the last century? (Andy Hunter, *The Mission*, December 16, 2001)

A Little Perspective

If we could shrink the earth's population to a village of precisely 100 people, with all the existing human ratios remaining the same, it would look something like this:

There would be 57 Asians, 21 Europeans, 14 from the Western Hemisphere, and 8 Africans.

Of those 100, there would be:
    52 females
    48 males
    70 nonwhite
    30 white
    70 non-Christian
    30 Christian
    89 heterosexual
    11 homosexual

6 people would possess 59% of the entire world's wealth. All 6 would be from the United States.

80 would live in substandard housing.

50 would not be able to read.

50 would suffer from malnutrition.

1 would be near death, 1 would be near birth.

1 would have a college education.

1 would own a computer. (*The Tie*, August 29, 2001)

A Useless Invention

"That's an amazing invention, but who would ever want to use one of them?" (Rutherford B. Hayes, 19th President of the United States, speaking to telephone inventor Alexander Graham Bell after participating in a trial telephone conversation between Washington and Philadelphia in 1876.)

Definition of Success

He has achieved success who has lived well, laughed often and loved much; who has enjoyed the trust of pure women, the respect of intelligent men and the love of little children; who has filled his niche and accomplished his task; who has left the world better than he found it, whether by an improved poppy, a perfect poem or a rescued soul; who has never lacked appreciation of earth's beauty or failed to express it; who has always looked for the best in others and given them the best he had; whose life was an inspiration; whose memory a benediction. (Bessie Anderson Stanley, 1904)

Is It The Right Thing To Do?

How can one decide what the ethically correct thing to do is? I have a personal four-point checklist I have used for years that I believe answers this question quite effectively.

1. Is it legal?

2. If someone else did "this" to you, would you think it was fair?

3. Would you be content if this were to appear on the front page of your hometown newspaper?

4. Would you like your mother to see you do this?

If you can answer "yes" to all four questions, then whatever you are about to do is probably ethical. (Norman Augustine, Chairman, Lockheed Martin, 1997)

Five Major Time Wasters

1. Spreading yourself too thin by trying to do too many things at once. You must set priorities for each day and, if necessary, each hour. Get the most important things done first.

2. Being afraid to delegate. Convince yourself that it's not necessary to do everything yourself. You can still be certain things are being done the way you want them to be when you delegate.

3. Not wanting to say "No" to requests. You can't say "yes" to everything without getting in over your head. Decide what you must do – and want to do – and say "no" to all other requests.

4. Being tied to the phone. Have others screen your calls. Use an answering machine when you don't want to be disturbed. Schedule a telephone hour to return calls.

5. Procrastinating. Get those unpleasant chores done first – if they're important. Divide large tasks into smaller ones. Reward yourself when you accomplish something. (Dr. Jan Yager, *Woman's Own*)

Everything Grows

Roberto Vacca observed, "Everything grows: everything is on the increase, and every year the speed of that increase is greater." With that in mind, consider the following:

1. In 1800 there were one billion people; in 1930, two billion; 1960, three billion; 1975, four billion; 1987, five billion; 1998, six billion.

2. Life expectancy worldwide was 21 years at the time of Christ; 48 years in 1955; and 65 years in 1995. This is expected to rise to 85 years by 2050.

3. We use seven times as much water as in 1900.

4. Paper consumption per capita in the United States tripled from 1940 to 1980, and tripled again in the next ten years (to 1800 pounds).

5. There are 62,000 new book titles and new editions each year.

6. In 1960, the average CEO traveled 12,000 miles per year. Today, the average CEO travels 112,000 miles per year.

7. The Physician Desk Reference had 300 pages when it first came out in 1948; fifty years later it has 3000 pages.

8. The NBA rulebook had two pages when basketball first started about one hundred years ago. It now has 114 pages.

9. In 1978 the average grocery store had 11,000 products. Today it has 30,000 products.

10. There are 550 different kinds of coffee, 250 different kinds of toothpaste, and 175 different kinds of salad dressing.

11. There are 2500 different types of light bulbs – in one store alone. (Dr. Richard A. Swenson, *Hurtling Toward Oblivion*)

Timely Words

For

Your Wallet

Money Smarts

Instead of putting larger purchases on credit, save the money first. Break down the cost of the item into a monthly sum you can put aside over a period of time. Once you have enough cash, make the purchase. Amazingly, by the time you save up the money, you may change your mind a dozen times. You might even decide you no longer need or want it.

When you write a check, round it up. Take the difference in change and deposit it each evening into a change jar at home or allow it to stay in your account to build a "pad." For example, if the bill comes to $33.02 write the check for $34 and stash the 98 cents in change. This does two things: First, you'll be amazed at how much change you'll accumulate in a year's time. Second, it makes reconciling your checkbook easier.

If you find yourself constantly borrowing money you've determined to save, here's one extreme way to put some space between you and your savings: Open your savings account in a bank in another city and make all of your deposits by mail.

Make savings a regular monthly bill. When you pay bills, write a check to your savings account or any other investment you may have. If you can't start with 10% of your gross income, start with a little and work your way up to at least 10%. (Mary Hunt, *Tiptionary*)

"We're better off financially if we always act our wage."

Seinfeld on Taxes

"Which is really crushing our lives more? Paying the taxes or doing the taxes? I think it's close. To me, the sad thing about doing your taxes is when you realize all you have to show for a whole year of activity is a shoebox full of receipts. Then I empty it out and start January 1 filling it up again. This is what I'm doing with my life. I'm filling up shoeboxes with little pieces of paper and showing it to the government.

I wish instead of doing my taxes I could just take my shoe box to Washington, D.C., right to the I.R.S., and just go, "Here, look. It's the same box as last year. Do we have to go through all this again?"

But what do I get for all the money I spend on taxes? I don't have any kids, I don't use the school system. I don't use the police, the prisons. I've never called the military. Basically, I use the post office and the white lines on the road. A third of my working life for postcards and driving straight." (Jerry Seinfeld, *SeinLanguage*)

"One way to pay less tax – earn less."

Money Mistake

In the summer of 1992, Boston Red Sox slugger Jack Clark filed for bankruptcy and announced that he was broke. His expensive hobbies of racing cars, home owning, and high living left him $1 million in debt. This financial failure came in spite of Clark's $3 million annual salary plus a $1.5 million signing bonus the previous year.

"Whoever loves money never has enough money; whoever loves wealth is never satisfied with his income." (Ecclesiastes 5:10)

Quotable

The fellow who waits for a break usually ends up broke.

A Better Risk

Instead of throwing away five or ten dollars a week on lottery tickets for the next forty years, invest that money in an aggressive mutual fund. Don't think that such an investment is risky. Investing in the lottery is the ultimate bad risk. Remember: The lottery is a tax on the ignorant. On the other hand, many mutual funds can get started with as little as $25.

"Dishonest money dwindles away, but he who gathers money little by little makes it grow." (Proverbs 13:11)

A Taxing Problem

At the time the federal income tax was established (1913), the typical taxpayer had to fork over about 8% of his income to Uncle Sam. Today, federal, state and local taxes siphon off around 40% of the average family's income – more than it spends in housing, food, and clothing combined.   (*Current Thoughts and Trends*, June 1999)

"An income tax refund is like being shot at and missed."

The G.O.K. Fund

Start a G.O.K. fund – God Only Knows. Saving into an emergency fund first is an essential element for financial peace. Financial planners advise that you should have at least three months salary tucked away in an emergency fund. Before you do that, however, become debt free. First, put $1000 in your G.O.K. fund. Then work toward paying off all debts except your mortgage. When your debts are paid, then you can build your G.O.K. fund for those unexpected events.   (Dave Ramsey, *Financial Peace*]

The Merits of Being a Miser

Warren Buffett, one of the richest and greatest investors of modern time, once said, "Most of the great investors are misers."

A trait many rich people share is frugalness. "Being frugal is the cornerstone of wealth-building," wrote Thomas Stanley, author of *The Millionaire Next Door.* He says most people have it all wrong about wealth in America. First of all, wealth is not the same as income. You can make a lot of money, but if you spend it all, you're not building wealth.

The problem is that the image most of us have of rich people is a distorted Hollywood version of flashy cars, designer dresses, sunglasses and exotic homes. But the truth is, most rich people in America don't live that way. Of the millionaires Stanley interviewed, most drove mid-level American-made cars and never bought expensive watches or shoes.

Most of the wealthy in this country make good, conscious decisions about every dollar they spend every day. Even the wealthiest men in history were tightwads. John D. Rockefeller would reuse the same tea bag several times before he threw it away. John Paul Getty used to charge his friends for phone calls when they came for long weekends on his estate. He would also wait until the last hours of the day to attend museums when admission was free!

The point is that you should not feel bad about brown bagging your lunch or reusing plastic bags and aluminum foil. Instead, let it stand as evidence that you are as smart as some of the richest men the world has ever known. Things such as home and car expenses, taxes, and insurance eat up 85% of your income. It's important to make the remaining 15% go a long way.

"The hand of the diligent makes rich." (Proverbs 10:4)

Hazardous Materialism

The great newspaper publisher, William Randolph Hearst, spent a great deal of his time collecting works of art. The story is told that one day he found a description of an artwork that he felt he must own. He employed an agent to find this particular piece of work. After months of searching, the agent reported to Mr. Hearst that the treasured work of art was in his warehouse along with many other valuable works that were still in their crates. Hearst had been searching for a treasure he already owned! Such is the power of wealth that it blinds us to the treasures we already have and focuses us on obtaining more, without appreciating what we have.

"Where your treasure is, there will your heart be also." (Matthew 6:21)

"How pleasant life would be if people with money used it the way the people who don't have any say they would spend it if they did."

Plasticless Shopping

Retailers are keenly aware of the statistics that prove you will spend at least 30 percent more if you are in the store with a credit card, debit card, or checkbook. The last thing they want is a customer who carries cash. Why? Because they know how cautious and nonimpulsive the cash buyer is. (Mary Hunt, *Tiptionary*)

Timely Thought

If you want to stay out of debt, you must earn more than you yearn.

Advice from a Sow

"A lot of people will urge you to put some money in a bank, and in fact – within reason – this is very good advice. But don't go overboard. Remember, what you are doing is giving your money to somebody else to hold on to, and I think it is worth keeping in mind that the people who run banks are so worried about holding on to things that they put little chains on all their pens." (Miss Piggy)

Hold On

The most common money management mistake made by Americans is withholding too much in taxes from your paycheck. That is like giving the IRS an interest-free loan. Ask your tax preparer to help you calculate the correct amount to withhold. (Stuart Kessler, CPA, *The Big Black Book*)

Reality Check

Ever wonder how much you are worth? Here's how to calculate your net worth. First, list all of your assets at their actual or estimated fair-market value. Then list all of your liabilities – all the money you owe, including credit card debt and mortgages. Your net worth is your total assets minus your total liabilities. Check it annually to monitor your progress.

Because it lists your assets and liabilities, a net worth statement can serve as a prepared financial statement when you apply for a loan and it's a good measure of your available emergency money. (Barbara O'Neill, *Saving on a Shoestring: How to Cut Expenses, Reduce Debt, Stash More Cash*)

"The safest way to double your money is to fold it over and put it in your pocket."

"The only place you can find financial security is inside your income."

"The kind of wealth most of us need isn't dollars but sense."

Car Fax

Want to know how to get the best possible price on a new car? Try this idea next time you're shopping for a new ride.

Fax a letter to all of the dealers in the area who sell the car you want. Specify exactly what you want, including all of the options. Include your fax number (but not your phone number) and invite them to fax you an itemized price offer. Give them a firm deadline by which to respond. Some dealers won't reply, but others will. Take the lowest bid and do one more round of faxing, inviting all the dealers to beat the best price you received. Then walk into the winning dealership with the firm offer. (*The Motley Fool*)

"Instruct a wise man and he will be wiser still; teach a righteous man and he will add to his learning." (Proverbs 9:9)

A Recipe for Greed

Many years ago, a major American company had trouble keeping employees working in their assembly plant in Panama. The laborers lived in a generally agrarian, barter economy, but the company paid them in cash. Since the average employee had more cash after a week's work than he had ever seen, he would periodically quit working, satisfied with what he had made.

What was the solution? Company executives gave all of their employees a Sears catalog. No one quit then, because they all wanted the previously undreamed of things they saw in the book.

It is difficult to save money when your neighbors keep buying things you can't afford.

Seven Keys To Financial Success

1) Value each and every penny.
2) Control every penny.
3) Save money.
4) Invest what you save.
5) Make money.

6) Protect your money.
7) Share your money. (Robert Allen)

Future Earnings

Know what you have coming to you. Call the Social Security Administration at 800-772-1213 for a "Request for Earnings and Benefits Estimate Statement." After you mail back the completed form, you will receive a statement showing all the money you have paid into social security as well as a personalized estimated monthly benefit upon retirement. If there are errors, such as they didn't credit you one year or they have you earning the wrong amount, they can be corrected but only if you report them. (Mary Hunt, *Tiptionary*)

By the time a man has money to burn, the fire has gone out.

If someone asks you for a loan, say you were just going to ask him for one. That usually ends the conversation.

Money is a good servant but a bad master.

Little Remedies for Money Headaches

In *The 15 Minute Money Manager,* Bob and Emilie Barnes offer these suggestions that can help when money is tight.

1. Hold a garage sale.
2. Sell any major drain on your cash flow. For example, a car, boat, or computer.
3. Check your life insurance to see if you have cash value you can borrow.
4. "Brown bag" instead of eating out. Five dollars a day for lunch equals over a hundred dollars per month.
5. Put your hobby to work.
6. Get an extra job.
7. Sell any collectibles that you might have.
8. Use extra money to pay off debts. Many people take a "windfall" and use it to get into deeper debt. For example, a tax refund is used to make a down payment on a new car. Instead of creating another monthly bill with extra cash, use it to pay down on debt.

Family Matters

Want to solve your problem of having too many relatives visiting? One man solved it by borrowing money from the rich ones and loaning it to the poor ones. Now none of his relatives come to see him.

Credit Card Facts

Today more than 31 million of the 211 million Visa and MasterCard cards in circulation are "affinity cards" – cards that donate a portion of each purchase to the charity shown on the card.

A dachshund named Alice once received four credit cards in the mail...without even asking (or barking) for it. One card promised that Alice would be welcomed as a "preferred customer" at one of Chicago's finest restaurants. (*Uncle John's Ultimate Bathroom Reader*)

Timely Trivia

The British monarchy costs taxpayers over $85 million a year.

One ounce of gold can be beaten thin enough to cover an entire acre of land.

Interesting Power

The power of compound interest is fascinating. Here's an example:

Ben, age 22, invests $1000 per year compounded annually at ten percent for eight years until he is thirty years old. For the next thirty-five years, until he is sixty-five, Ben invests not one penny more.

Arthur, age 30, invests $1000 per year for thirty-five years until he is sixty-five years old. His investment also earns ten percent compound interest per year. At age sixty-five, will Arthur or Ben have the most money?

Ben will have $388,865 while Arthur will have $329,039. (Dave Ramsey, *Financial Peace*)

Expensive Habits

A person who smokes cigarettes at a moderate rate would save over $1000 per year if they were to quit. In addition, future medical bills will likely be reduced also. (Mary Hunt, *Tiptionary*)

A five dollar lunch bought every weekday of the year for fifty weeks – (two weeks off for vacation) – adds up to $1250 per year.

Setting your air conditioning thermostat at 72° will cost you 30% more than a setting of 78°.

The Money Maker

The Small Business Administration reported recently that a new American millionaire is created every 22 minutes. That equals about 75 new millionaires a day!

Someone has said that when one becomes wealthy, God gets a partner or the man loses his soul.

But wealth should be a reminder of God's goodness to us, not a suggestion to stray from Him.

The Bible says, "Remember the Lord your God, for it is He who gives you the ability to produce wealth" (Deuteronomy 8:18).

Think you're not wealthy? Consider the fact that most people in the world live in small, simple homes or huts, own only a few articles of clothing, and eat one meager meal a day. Of the six billion people on the planet, we in America are blessed. Don't let anyone fool you. You're rich!

Toward Your Wealth

In their book, *The 15-Minute Money Manager*, Bob and Emilie Barnes share four secrets for developing financial strength:

1) Earn little by little. Proverbs 13:11 says, "He who gathers money little by little makes it grow." Develop a life of being satisfied with a little at a time while having a consistent savings plan.

2) Save little by little. A small amount set aside on a regular basis grows faster than you may think.

3) Share your blessings. It's important to be able to share a portion of what you've been blessed with.

4) Stay out of debt. You can either earn interest or pay interest. Which would you rather do?

"A faithful man will abound with blessings." (Proverbs 28:20)

Lessons From a Farmer

In his book, *Money Lessons for a Lifetime*, Jim Jorgensen tells this story:

Much of what I learned about how to accumulate wealth and build a cash reserve came from talking with farmers.

If I had to wrap up all the financial planning ideas in the world, they could be boiled down to one simple premise told to me over a hayrake in an equipment store:

Save some money the safe way and then take some risks for the years ahead.

That's the whole deal and it worked for the farmers. Everyone in our small town knew they were rich. They paid cash and they drove big Cadillacs.

So I asked one of these farmers, "How did you save money and get so rich?"

"Well, sonny," he said, looking me straight in the eyes, "if you don't pay yourself first, no one else will."

"Is that all there is to getting rich?" I asked.

"That's it," he said. "Lord knows you don't have to be smart. You don't have to make a lot of money. But if you don't save *some* money each month, all the fancy investment advice in the world won't make you rich. Remember, nobody has ever gone broke with money in the bank."

That kind of makes you want to stop what you're doing and go put some money in the bank, doesn't it?

Baby Steps

The following is a brief outline of the seven "baby steps" to financial peace by author and bankruptcy counselor, Dave Ramsey:

1) Pay the minimum on all debts until you have $1000 in savings.

2) Pay off all personal debt except your home. Pay off the smallest balance first. When that is paid off, pay off the next one by paying the minimum plus the amount you were paying on the first one. This will create a "snowball" effect until all debts are paid.

3) After all debts except your home are paid, save three to six months of your expenses.

4) Begin your retirement savings.

5) Start a college fund if necessary.

6) Pay off your mortgage early. Apply extra money toward the principal.

7) Build your wealth. Be a philanthropist. Give your money away. (Dave Ramsey, *Financial Peace*)

Moneywise

Money will buy a fine dog, but only love will make him wag his tail.

There's a new golden rule in effect today: "He who has the gold, makes up the rules."

Money is the number one cause of domestic unhappiness. Many couples need to undergo plastic surgery. They need to have their credit cards cut up.

Nowadays people can be divided into three classes: the Haves, the Have-Nots, and the Have-Not-Paid-for-What-They-Haves.

"For the love of money is a root of all kinds of evil. Some people, eager for money, have wandered from the faith and pierced themselves with many griefs." (1 Timothy 6:10)

Minimum Impact

If you charge $1000 to your credit card and pay just the minimum monthly requirement, it could take you more than 20 years to pay back that $1000 – and you will have paid about $2000 in interest along the way. (Andrew Tobias)

Third World Materialism

Author Ron Blue tells the story of visiting a small, rural village in Africa. Ron asked a native there what the biggest problem was facing his village. The man said, "Materialism."

Ron was taken aback. He expected it to be the lack of food or medical attention or perhaps problems with neighboring villages. But materialism? These villagers didn't have televisions or cars or satellite dishes – the sorts of things we associate with "the good life."

But this villager told Ron, "If a man has a mud hut, he wants one made out of stone. If he has a thatch roof, he wants a tin roof. If he has one acre, he wants two. Materialism is a disease of the heart. It has nothing to do with where you live."

"Stuffitis" – the disease of always wanting more, better, and newer stuff, infects all cultures.

"Seek first the kingdom of God and His righteousness and all these things will be given to you." (Matthew 6:33)

One More Bill

Add another person to your long list of bills to be paid: you. Pay yourself monthly just like you pay any other bill. Put money away each month in a savings account, or better yet, a mutual fund. Many mutual funds can be started with as little as $25 a month.

Money Myths

Here are a few financial tips from Mary Hunt's book, *Tiptionary:*

Myth: Buying things on sale is a great way to save money. Truth: Buying things on sale is a way to spend less money, but it has absolutely nothing to do with saving money.

Stop trying to impress people. If you can stop spending according to demands put on your life by others (through peer pressure or the necessity to keep up), you will see a tremendous difference in the way you spend. (Besides, most people are so self-centered they don't pay attention to you anyway!)

Money Miracle

It's been called the "eighth wonder of the world." It is more commonly known as compound interest. Here are a couple of examples:

If you accumulate $10,000 in a savings account in the next four years and then let it grow at an eight percent interest rate for the next forty years, it will be worth $217,245.

Suppose you could put away $2000 a year for forty years. At eight percent interest, you would have $518,113. At twelve percent, you would have $1.5 million.

Money Strategy

The following ten money strategies are recommended by Michael Stolper, President of Stolper and Company, an investment advisory firm.

1) Weigh every purchase based on a cost/benefit analysis.
2) Put discretionary money to work.
3) Prefund life's big expenses, such as college education.
4) Pay down your mortgage.
5) Participate in your company's 401(k) program if it has one or set up an IRA.
6) Sign up for a monthly automatic transfer from your bank account to a mutual fund.
7) Buy a cash-value life insurance policy to build up some assets.
8) Take out a bank loan to make an investment.
9) Don't borrow money to pay for assets that have little value.
10) Figure out how much money you need to get from here to there. Affluent people do not suddenly wonder how they are going to pay for their 16-year-old's college tuition.

Giving Pays

One morning while swimming, young Winston Churchill started to drown. Luckily, Alexander Fleming was nearby to rescue Churchill.

Knowing that Fleming wished to be a doctor, Winston Churchill's father decided to finance his education for saving his son's life.

Years later, when Prime Minister Churchill lay dying of pneumonia, Dr. Fleming was called to treat him.   Using penicillin that he had discovered, he cured Churchill.

How true are the words of King Solomon in Ecclesiastes 11:1, "Give generously, for your gifts will return to you later" (*Seeds From The Sower*)

Interesting Tip

If you have an interest bearing checking account (which you should), don't pay bills until they are due. If the due date for your $150 power bill is the 15th of the month, why pay it on the 1st when you can let that money earn interest for two more weeks?

Poor Retirement Plan

A survey by the Consumer Federation of America and Primerica financial services reports that 40% of Americans who make $35,000 a year or less believe that their best chance to build wealth for retirement is by playing the lottery rather than patiently saving and investing.   Many Americans don't understand the basics of how small amounts of money can grow tremendously when invested over time.

The chances of winning big in the lottery are 10 to 20 million to 1. The chance of becoming a millionaire by investing small amounts of money each month is a sure bet.   If a 25 year-old invests $30 a month into a good mutual fund or stock, it will turn into $1 million by the time he/she is 65. If you're 30, you need only invest $70 a month.

Wise Thinking

A man is wise who does not grieve for the things which he has not, but rejoices for the things which he has.   Continually compare what you want with what you have, and you will be unhappy.   Instead, compare what you deserve with what you have, and you'll be happy. (John Mason)

"The world and its desires pass away, but the man who does the will of God lives forever." (1 John 2:17)

Big Mistakes

Paying too much interest on a high credit card balance...not raising the deductible on homeowner's and auto insurance policies to at least $500...neglecting to write a will...not putting as much money as possible into a tax-deferred retirement savings account. (Alexandra Armstrong, Certified Financial Planner, *Handbook of Inside Information*)

Five Get-Out-of Debt-Fast Secrets

The average U.S. household carries $5600 in credit card debt on eleven different cards. The first step to getting out of the hole is stop digging deeper. Use these five proven methods to end your credit card debt forever.

1. *Sleep on it.* Make yourself a promise. When you find something you want to purchase that costs more than $50, don't. Give it 24 hours. Ask yourself three questions: Do I really need it? Will it make me happier or my life easier? Is this the cheapest way to do this? Buy only if you can answer "yes" to all three questions.

2. *Pay Cash for Twinkies and Gas.* Using credit cards for gas, food, and utilities is an easy way to pump up your debt. These items should be budgeted as fixed expenses and paid for with cash. If this isn't working, try keeping receipts for everything you buy for one month. Then you'll know how much to budget out of every paycheck.

3. *Forget Your Plastic.* Next time you're in the market for something expensive like a TV or sofa, try saving for it. Put away twenty or thirty dollars every month until you've got enough cash. You'll be surprised how much better you are at finding bargains when you pay with your own hard-earned cash.

4. *Forget No-Interest Plans.* These are the deals you see at appliance and jewelry stores in which you pay nothing down and make no payments for another year or so. The problem is,

if you miss a payment, all the finance charges accrued since the purchase date will be due – sometimes these are as high as 20%.

5. *Barter For It.* Start by trading for one thing a month. Babysit for your neighbors one night in exhange for the same service for your kids the next. Trade your carpentry skills for free legal advice or the use of your chain saw for a ride to the airport. There's no limit to what you can barter – and how much extra cash you can pocket. (Brett Saso, *The National Fair Credit Service*)

Baboons and Stewardship

A television documentary on animal life in Africa was demonstrating how the natives of Africa have learned to find water during the dry season. A native would first locate a colony of baboons. Sure that the baboons were watching, the African dug a small hole in a dirt embankment. He then placed a handful of fruit inside. Baboons, it seems, are incurably curious, so as soon as the native returned into the jungle, one baboon quickly approached the hole. Seeing the fruit inside, the baboon stuck his hand in the hole and grasped the tasty morsel. The African hunter had skillfully carved the hole just large enough to allow the animal's hand to enter but, when clasped around the fruit, the hand could not be withdrawn.

The native then returned from the concealment of the forest with a small rope in his hands. Amazingly, as the man approached, the baboon shrieked in terror, but refused to release the fruit and run for its life.

I found myself moving to the edge of my chair as this drama intensified. I wanted to shout to the baboon, "Let go and run for your life!" But the native casually strolled up to the panic-stricken animal, laid the noose over the animal's neck, and pulled him away. The animal was then tied to a tree, given salt, and held captive for a couple of days without water. As soon as it was released, the baboon made a beeline for its secret waterhole. The native simply followed the thirst-driven animal and found the water he would never have found without the animal's unwitting assistance.

As I watched this drama unfold, I was impressed with the hunter's wisdom, humored by the comical simplicity of it, but mortified to see myself in the story. I thought, "This is not a story about a baboon and water; this is a story about me and the foolishness of my own behavior!" How often have I, as the rational and intelligent being that God made me to be, performed precisely the same behavior as the baboon? Adam and Eve lost the garden for one bite. Esau sold his birthright for one meal. Samson traded his special gift of strength for a woman.

How easily have I been overcome with the enticement of a fist full of fruit! What price tag is attached to selfish attitudes and action?

In the long run, a lifestyle of "getting" and "grabbing" is exceedingly more costly than a life of "giving." I had wanted to warn the baboon, "Let go!" and yet, how often have I, myself, failed to accept the same advice? (Don Linscott, *The Genesis Group, Winter 2000 Newsletter*)

Bright Stars in Used Cars

When financial planner Jonathan Pond uses a shovel to scrape the snow off his used 1986 Toyota, his neighbors watch in horror. His 12-year-old daughter eventually adjusted, but for a while was mortified when he drove her to a friend's house or to school in his old Cadillac. She asked to be dropped off a block away.

"People laugh at my cars. Who cares?" said Pond, a nationally known public television and radio commentator and author. He credits his used car buying habit with helping to build his family's net worth to more than a million dollars.

Dan Bradley, a retirement planning specialist, bought a five-year-old Plymouth Neon with $7000 cash rather than use it as a down payment on a new $22,000 Buick. When he did the math, he discovered that he could have an extra $37,000 in five years by investing the difference.

"I'm turning fifty this year. I realize it's not the car you drive," but other things, such as the ability to afford a nicer house, pay for your children's college education, and save for retirement.

Pond and Bradley aren't the only financially savvy people who say there are better ways to use your money than buying a new expensive car every few years, or leasing something you can't afford to own. To name a few:

- Andrew Tobias, author of "The Only Investment Guide You'll Ever Need" and used car buyer, says "That new car smell is the most expensive fragrance in the world."

- Paul Kangas, co-anchor of the "Nightly Business Report," is currently driving a 1983 Chevrolet Caprice with 150,000 miles.

- Lawrence Coolidge, senior trustee of Loring, Wolcott and Coolidge, a Boston investment firm says, "Old cars produce cheap transportation. I'd rather give the money away to Jobs for Youth than buy a $50,000 Land Rover," referring to a Boston non-profit organization.

According to Pond's calculations, over a 40-year working career, a person who buys a new car and keeps it for ten years can come out financially ahead of someone who trades in for a new car every three years. According to the study, if that person takes the savings in new-car payments and insurance and invests it, allowing the money to compound over the decades, the total would be about $385,000. Enough to help fund an early retirement. (*Saving and Spending News, MSN MoneyCentral*)

Debt Free

Approximately 80 percent of all Americans have negative net worth (which means they owe more than they are worth). When you spend more than you make, the result is debt. Once you've gotten into debt, how do you get out?

1) Recognize there is no easy way out of debt. Getting out of debt takes planning, discipline, work, and time.

2) Try to increase your income.

3) Avoid impulse buying.

4) Shop comparatively.

5) Use your credit cards intelligently. Pay the balance off each month.

6) Buy quality. Cheap goods aren't always economical.

7) Develop moneymaking hobbies.

8) Begin to pay off debt. Pay off the debt with the highest interest rate first. Then pay off the next one and include the amount you were paying on the first. Continue this until all debts are paid.

9) Begin to prevent future debt. As you pay off one debt, don't go back into debt for something else. Build a savings account to provide a cushion for emergencies and special purchases.

Somebody's Gotta Do It

Express Personnel Services of Oklahoma City says its informal poll proves there's a job for everybody. Some examples, including hourly pay:
- Wipe blood and other body fluids from Plexiglas at hockey games, $7
- Chase deer off an airport runway, $8
- Pour thousands of cans of rancid beer down a drain, $6

Express found a company in Redmond, WA that hired three temps to look busy and professional to make visitors think it had a larger staff. The appearance of working paid $11 an hour. (*The Augusta Chronicle*, March 11, 2001)

Quotables

"What is considered a living wage depends on whether you pay it or get it."

"Bank accounts give a person a good feeling. Until he realizes they are insured by an agency of a federal government that's three trillion dollars in debt." (*The Indianapolis News*)

"I don't know what makes the stock market work. I wasn't an economics major." (Steve Jobs, CEO, Apple)

When We Give, We Thrive

Eighty years ago, the religious philosopher, Harry Emerson Fosdick, wrote about one river feeding two seas, the Sea of Galilee and the Dead Sea. The Sea of Galilee takes in water and "makes beauty of it, for the Sea of Galilee has an outlet. It gets to give. It gathers in its riches that it may pour them out again to fertilize the Jordan plain. But the Dead Sea with the same water makes horror. For the Dead Sea has no outlet. It gets to keep."

In Fosdick's words, when we give we thrive, when we keep it, we begin to die. This is neither hypothesis nor hyperbole, it is truth. Giving is that important. And the proof rings like Fosdick's river through the history of man. (Harvey Drucker, Argonne National Laboratory)

Three Ways to Win With Pushy Salespeople

Salespeople are conditioned to close the sale – sometimes before you're sure what you want to do. Here are some assertive, honest remarks that can defuse the pressure.

1. "I'm not buying today, but if I decide to buy, I'll ask for you." When salespeople are on commission, they worry that they'll do all the work and someone else will make the sale – and the money. State this up front, and you'll get a more valuable interaction than you would if you said, "I'm just looking."

2. "I have a very strict financial plan, and I need to see if these payments will fit in with it." This remark portrays you as financially responsible without giving the salesperson false hopes. Don't misrepresent yourself with a statement like "I probably can't afford this." If it's true, it's nobody's business. If not, it undermines your negotiating power.

3. "I just won't buy on impulse. It's too much hassle to return things. I'll come back if I decide I want this." This comment serves as a gentle reminder that you won't be pressured into buying until you're sure you want the item, and it reinforces the idea that you will return an item that doesn't suit you. It works much better than a lame remark such as "I'm not sure about pink."

Become a Professional Handyman

So you're not a professional painter or wallpaper hanger, but you're not a complete klutz either? If you're pretty good with a hammer or paintbrush, here's how you can turn your work into savings. Every time your house needs work – carpentry, painting, plumbing, wallpapering – for which you have the skills, do it yourself. But here's the important part: Pay yourself for the job. Determine how much it would cost to hire a professional, then pay yourself the going rate by depositing the amount in your savings account. (If you can't afford the going rate for a particular service, pay yourself half.) When you really need to hire someone – say, to put on a new roof – the money will be waiting for you.

It All Started When...

These five companies started in a garage or kitchen table and ended up as household names.

1. In 1976, buddies Steve Jobs and Steve Wozniak were on the verge of starting the personal computer revolution. For their first order of 50 Apple Computers, they bought parts on credit and spent marathon sessions soldering Jobs's garage.

2. The Avon lady, mother of all door-to-door sales representatives, was originally a man. In 1886, David McConnell, a door-to-door book salesman from Suffern, New York, gave away as a sales premium vials of perfume that he and a chemist friend mixed themselves. The rest is history.

3. In January 1910, Joyce Hall arrived in Kansas City, Missouri, with two shoeboxes full of picture postcards. From his base at the local YMCA (where he stored his inventory under his bed), he set up a mail-order business that evolved into Hallmark, the world-famous greeting card company.

4. In the mid-1950's, Bette Nesmith Graham was a secretary with a problem. She was a poor typist who couldn't erase mistakes when she typed with the new electric typewriters. She decided that what she couldn't erase, she'd cover up – with a white, water-based paint. Graham's invention was so popular with other secretaries that she mixed up batches of Mistake Out in her kitchen and garage for them. In 1979, she sold the Liquid Paper Company for $47.5 million.

5. It was 1899 and Joshua Lionel Cowen had just invented a method by which flash powder could be ignited by using dry cell batteries to hit a wire fuse. The U.S. Navy offered him $12,000

to develop this process for electrically charged mine exploration. Cowen took those earnings and opened his own company to create an electric fan and a flashlight. However, noticing a toy train display in a ship window, Cowen experienced a "eureka" moment. The poor toys sat lifeless, devoid of excitement. Wouldn't it help attract business if the displays presented continuous motion?

Cowen went back to his shop and set to work. Beginning with a rectangular wooden box, he affixed the motor from his failed fan invention, attached insulated metal wheels, constructed a metal track set in wooden ties and wired dry cell batteries right into the track. He stained the wooden box red, stenciled on it Electric Express, sold it to that same shop and Lionel trains were born.

Pampering the Furnace
(Do not try this at home.)

Charlie MacArthur of Sangerville, Maine, thought he'd figured out the best way to reuse solid waste when he built a car engine that would run on chicken fat. Then when his children came along, he had a better idea. He modified his furnace to burn dirty diapers. Not only did the invention reduce his heating bill, but it also cut down on trips to the dump. (*Living Well on a Shoestring*, p. 98)

Top Ten Things to Know About Making a Budget

1. Budgets are a necessary evil.

They're the only practical way to get a grip on your spending so you can make sure your money is used the way you want it.

2. Creating a budget generally requires three steps.

They are: 1) identify how you spend money now, 2) evaluate that spending and set goals that take into account your financial objectives, and 3) track your spending to make sure it stays within those guidelines.

3. Use software to save grief.

If you use a personal-finance program such as Quicken or Microsoft Money, the built-in budget-making tools can create your budget for you.

4. Don't drive yourself nuts.

One drawback of monitoring your spending by computer is that it encourages overzealous attention to detail. Once you determine which categories of spending can and should be cut (or expanded), concentrate on those categories and worry less about other aspects of your spending.

5. Watch out for cash leakage.

If withdrawals from the ATM machine evaporate from your pocket without apparent explanation, it's time to keep better records. In general, any time cash expenses exceed 5 percent of your total spending, they need to be checked.

6. Spending beyond your limits is dangerous.

If so, you've got plenty of company. Government figures show that many households with total income of $50,000 or less are spending more than they bring in. This doesn't make you an automatic candidate for bankruptcy -- but it's definitely a sign you need to make some serious spending cuts.

7. Beware of luxuries dressed as necessities.

If your income doesn't cover your costs, then some of your spending is probably for luxuries -- even if you've been considering them to be filling a real need.

8. Tithe to yourself.

Aim to spend no more than 90 percent of your income. That way, you'll have the other 10 percent left to save for your big-picture items.

9. Don't count on windfalls.

When projecting the amount of money you can live on, don't include dollars that you can't be sure you'll receive, such as year-end bonuses, tax refunds or investment gains.

10. Beware of spending creep.

As your annual income climbs from raises, promotions and smart investing, don't start spending for luxuries until you're sure that you're staying ahead of inflation. (www.money.cnn.com)

Rules for Giving to Charity

1. The cause must be worthy. You want your gift dollars to go to objects thoroughly worthwhile.

2. You want to give as you *want* to give, voluntarily, cheerfully – without constraint or coercion.

3. You should be convinced in your own mind that there is a real, actual need.

4. Give where your money will reach the farthest. Make those gift dollars get the greatest results possible. Invest for time and eternity.

5. The administration of your gifts should be trustworthy. Your hard-earned money must not be wasted, dissipated, or wrongly used.

6. Avoid putting your gifts into any institution where the overhead is too large.

7. Give as you pray. If you cannot pray about it, don't give to it.

Timely Words

For

Your Funny Bone

Medical Mischief

Things you'd rather not hear in surgery:

- "Better save that part. We might need it later."
- "We're going to need a mop."
- "Accept this sacrifice, O Lord of Darkness."
- "Come back with that! Bad dog!"
- "Wait a minute! If this is his spleen, then what's that?"
- "The floor's clean, right?"
- "You know, there's big money in kidneys. Heck, the guy's got two of them."
- "That's cool! Now, can you make his leg twitch?" (Bill Kirby, *The Augusta Chronicle*, May 7, 1999)

Whoops!

Take heart in the fact that everybody makes mistakes:

In 1962, David Rowe, a Decca Record Co. employee was badgered by a friend to listen to a tape of an unknown pop music band. "I'm sorry..." he said after hearing it, "groups with guitars are on the way out." *The Beatles* had to go someplace else.

Actress Lana Turner's grandfather once owned a half share in a small company that made soft drinks. He sold out because he thought the name, *Coca-Cola*, wasn't catchy.

In 1972, a young film director named George Lucas tried to peddle an idea for a low-budget movie about teenagers in the early '60's. All the big companies rejected him. Universal, which earlier had rejected it, decided to take a chance. The film, *American Graffiti*, made millions.

You would think Lucas had everyone's attention when he made the rounds four years later with a new film idea about an outer space movie. But he received the same answers. Nobody wanted it.

Somehow he scraped up the money to make *Star Wars*, which grossed $134 million in its first four months.

"Things could be worse. Suppose your errors were counted and published each day, like those of a baseball player."

Headlines
(Actual headlines taken from newspapers around the country)

Include Your Children When Baking Cookies

Police Begin Campaign to Run Down Jaywalkers

Safety Experts Say School Bus Passengers Should Be Belted

Drunk Gets Nine Months in Violin Case

Survivor of Siamese Twins Joins Parents

Iraqi Head Seeks Arms

Panda Mating Fails; Veterinarian Takes Over

Lung Cancer in Women Mushrooms

Teachers Strike Idle Kids

Enraged Cow Injures Farmer with Ax

Riddle

Mahatma Gandhi walked barefoot most of the time, and produced an impressive set of calluses on his feet. He also ate very little, which made him rather frail and with his odd diet, he suffered from bad breath. This made him what?

Answer: A super callused fragile mystic plagued with halitosis.

Sermon Notes

The preacher was completing a sermon on the evils of alcohol. With great emotion he cried out, "If I had all the beer in the world, I'd take it and throw it into the river!"

With even greater emphasis he said, "And if I had all the wine in the world, I'd take it and throw it into the river!!"

Finally, he wailed, "And if I had all the whiskey in the world, I'd take it and throw it into the river!" Then he prayed and sat down.

The song leader stood and announced, "Our closing hymn is number 385, 'Shall We Gather At The River.'"

Up, Up, and Away
(Actual announcements made by airline flight crews during the pre-flight safety lecture)

"There may be fifty ways to leave your lover but there are only four ways to leave this plane."

"Your seat cushions can be used for floatation, and in the event of an emergency water landing, please take them with our compliments."

"Should the cabin lose pressure, oxygen masks will drop from the overhead area. Please place the bag over your own mouth and nose before assisting children or adults acting like children."

"We do feature a smoking section on this flight. If you must smoke, contact a member of the flight crew and we will escort you to the wing of the airplane." (*FYI: Georgia Views and News*)

Elevator Torture

Things to do on an elevator:

- Ask if you can push the button for other people, but push the wrong ones.
- Call the Psychic Hotline from a cell phone and ask if they know what floor you're on.
- Lay down a Twister mat and ask people if they'd like to play.
- Pretend you're a flight attendant and review emergency procedures and exits with the passengers.
- When the doors close, announce to the others, "Don't panic! They will open up again."
- Call out, "Group hug!" then enforce it.
- Stare, grinning at another passenger for a while, and then announce, "I have new socks on."
- Bring a camera and take pictures of everyone in the elevator.
- Swat at flies that don't exist.

Soothsaying

1. Pick a number from 2 to 9. It can be 2 or it can be 9, or any number in between.
2. Take the number that you've chosen and multiply it by 9.
3. That should give you a two-digit number. Take those two digits and add them together.
4. Take the resulting number and subtract 5 from it.
5. Take that number and correspond it to the alphabet, numbering the letters. A equals 1, B equals 2, etc.
6. Take your letter and think of a country that begins with that letter.
7. Take the last letter in the name of the country and think of an animal that begins with that letter.
8. Take the last letter in the name of that animal and think of a color.
9. But always remember that there are no orange kangaroos in Denmark. (Bill Kirby, *The Augusta Chronicle*, August 15, 1999)

Job Woes

The following are actual quotes taken from Federal Employee Performance Evaluations:

"Since my last report, this employee has reached rock bottom and has started to dig."

"His men would follow him anywhere, but only out of morbid curiosity."

"I would not allow this employee to breed."

"This employee is really not so much of a has been, but more of a definite won't be."

"Works well when under constant supervision and cornered like a rat in a trap."

"He would be out of his depth in a parking lot puddle."

Say What?

In South Carolina, voters participated in a referendum on revocation of local blue laws. The ballot question read:

"Shall the prohibition on Sunday work continue in this county subject to an employee's right to elect not to work on Sunday if the prohibition is not continued after certification of the result of this referendum to the Secretary of State?" (James J. Kilpatrick, *The Writer's Art*)

Old Timers

Old skiers never die – they just go downhill.

Old teachers never die – they just lose their class.

Old funeral directors never die – they just go underground.

Old truckers never die – they just lose their drive.

Old bowlers never die – they just end up in the gutter.

Old singers never die – they just lose their tune.

Old doctors never die – they just lose their patients.

Old mailmen never die – they just lose their zip.

Old bakers never die – they just fail to rise.

Old joggers never die – they just run down.

Old florists never die – they just wither away.

Old school principals never die – they just lose their faculties.

Old football players never die – they just fumble away.

Old gluttons never die – they just waist away. (Croft M. Pentz, *The Complete Book of Zingers*)

Work

Employees in a Detroit business office found the following important notice on the bulletin board: "The management regrets that it has come to their attention that workers dying on the job are failing to fall down. This practice must stop, as it becomes impossible to distinguish between death and the natural movement of the staff. Any employee found dead in an upright position will be dropped from the payroll."

Wise Advice from Kids

- Never trust a dog to watch your food. Patrick, age 10

- When your dad is mad and asks you, "Do I look stupid?" don't answer him. Michael, 14

- Never tell your mom her diet's not working. Michael, 14

- Stay away from prunes. Randy, 9

- Don't squat with your spurs on. Noronha, 13

- When your mom is mad at your dad, don't let her brush your hair. Taylia, 11

- Never allow your three year-old brother in the same room as your school assignment. Traci, 14

- Never hold a dust buster and a cat at the same time. Kyoyo, 9

- If you want a kitten, start out by asking for a horse. Naomi, 15

- Felt markers are not good to use as lipstick. Lauren, 9

- Never try to baptize a cat. Eileen, 8 (*FYI: Georgia Views and News*, September 1999)

Cowboy Wisdom
(A cowboy's guide to life)

1. Don't interfere with something that ain't botherin' you none.

2. The easiest way to eat crow is while it's still warm. The colder it gets, the harder it is to swaller.

3. If you find yourself in a hole, the first thing to do is stop diggin'.

4. Never ask a barber if you need a haircut.

5. Generally, you ain't learnin' nothin' when your mouth's a jawin'.

6. Good judgment comes from experience and a lotta that comes from bad judgment.

7. Lettin' the cat outta the bag is a whole lot easier than puttin' it back.

8. Never miss a good chance to shut up.

9. The biggest troublemaker you'll probably ever have to deal with watches you shave his face in the mirror every morning.

10. If it don't seem like it's worth the effort, it probably ain't.

Definitions

Buffet: A French word that means "get up and get it yourself."

Tattoo: Permanent proof of temporary insanity.

Celebrity Quotes

"I've been on a calendar, but I've never been on time." (Marilyn Monroe)

"Imagination is more important than knowledge." (Albert Einstein)

"Next week there can't be any crisis. My schedule is already full." (Henry Kissinger)

"I always wanted to be somebody but I should have been more specific." (Lily Tomlin)

"You've got to be very careful if you don't know where you are going because you might not get there." (Yogi Berra)

"Death is nature's way of saying, 'Your table is ready.'" (Robin Williams)

"Don't go around saying the world owes you a living. The world owes you nothing. It was here first." (Mark Twain)

Top Ten Things You Shouldn't Say to a Police Officer

1. Sorry, Officer, I didn't realize my radar detector wasn't plugged in.

2. Aren't you the guy from the Village People?

3. Hey, you must've been doin' about 125 to keep up with me. Good job!

4. Are you Andy or Barney?

5. I thought you had to be in relatively good physical condition to be a policeman.

6. You're not gonna check the trunk, are you?

7. I pay your salary!

8. Gee, Officer, thanks! The last officer only gave me a warning too!

9. I was trying to keep up with traffic. Yes, I know there are no other cars around. That's how far ahead of me they are.

10. Gee, Officer, your eyes look glazed. Have you been eating doughnuts? (*FYI: Georgia Views & News*, October 1999)

Remote Control

In St. Petersburg, Russia, zoo officials implemented a plan to introduce orangutans to the joys of family life by having them watch television together. The scheme backfired, however, because the male orangutan soon got so engrossed in TV that his mate became jealous and upset. The zoo director announced they would reduce the hours of television watching in an attempt to salvage the relationship. (*Current Thoughts & Trends*, April 1999)

No Respect

"We sleep in separate rooms, we have dinner apart, we take separate vacations – we're doing everything we can to keep our marriage together."

"I once asked my father if things were bad for him during the Depression. He said the first six months were bad, then he got used to me." *(Rodney Dangerfield)*

Timely Questions

Why do drugstores make the sick walk all the way to the back of the store to get a prescription while the healthy people can buy cigarettes at the front?

Why do banks leave both doors wide open and then chain pens to the counter?

Why do we leave cars worth thousands of dollars in the driveway and put useless junk in the garage?

Why do they have drive-up ATM's with Braille lettering?

Why did kamikaze pilots wear helmets?

Rivalry

On the American frontier, denominational differences were taken seriously. The story is told of a young Methodist minister who was asked to conduct a funeral for a Baptist. Since ministers were in short supply and he was the only one for miles around, he was unsure what to do. He performed the funeral and wrote to his bishop, asking if he had made the right decision and requesting some general guidelines for the future. His bishop's reply was brief. "Bury all the Baptists you can."

Thought for the Day

The cheapest way to have your family tree traced is to run for public office.

A Redneck's Famous Last Words

"Hey ya'll, watch this!"

"Gimme a match. I think my gas tank is empty."

(To his wife) "These biscuits are hard as a rock."

"Let's see if it's loaded."

"Step on it, boy, you're only going 80."

"If you knew anything, you wouldn't be a cop."

"Lemme have that bottle, I'll try it."

"Say, who's in charge here anyway?"

Quality Control

The owner of a drugstore overheard a young boy talking on a pay telephone. "Hello, sir, I was calling to see if you needed a lawn boy. Oh, you have one. Well, is he adequate? Oh, he is. Thank you, I was just checking." Then he hung up.

The druggist said to the boy, "Sorry you didn't get the job."

"Oh no, sir," the boy replied. "I've got the job. I was just calling to check up on myself."

Marriage Thoughts

"How long have you two been married?" asked a friend.

"We've been happily married for seven years," answered the husband. "Seven out of sixteen isn't bad."

Why do brides buy their wedding gowns and grooms rent their suits?

There's one word for a man who marries a rich woman – smart.

Pew Endurance

First church member: "I thought the sermon was divine. It reminded me of the peace of God."
Second church member: "I thought it passed all understanding."
Third church member: "It reminded me of the mercies of God. I thought it would endure forever."

Marital Bliss

A husband told his friend, "My wife and I had a fight last night."
"How did it end?" asked the friend.
"She came crawling to me on her hands and knees," he answered.
"Oh?" asked the friend. "What did she say?"
"Well," the husband reluctantly replied, she said, "Come out from under the bed, you coward!"

What Every Man Wants

She will always be beautiful and cheerful. She could marry a movie star, but wants only you. She will have hair that never needs curlers or beauty shops. Her beauty won't run in a rainstorm. She will never be sick – just allergic to jewelry and fur coats. She will be an expert in cooking, cleaning house, fixing the car, painting the house, and keeping quiet. She will hate charge cards.

email Humor
(Stuff found in my email)

I'm not into working out. My philosophy is no pain, no pain.
I am in shape. Round is a shape.

Do illiterate people get the full effect of alphabet soup?

Anybody going slower than you is an idiot. Anybody going faster than you is a maniac.

My grandmother started walking five miles a day when she was 60. She's 97 today and we don't know where she is.

One out of every four Americans suffers from some form of mental illness. Think of your three best friends. If they're okay, then it's you.

TV commercials show us how detergents take out bloodstains. I think if you've got a T-shirt with a bloodstain all over it, maybe laundry isn't your biggest problem.

The Devil You Say

One bright, beautiful Sunday morning, the congregation had just settled in for the morning service at church. Suddenly, the devil himself appeared at the front of the church. Everyone started screaming and racing toward the front door to get away from the evil menace.

Everyone except one gentleman, who sat calmly in his pew, not moving.

The author of confusion was confused himself. "Don't you know who I am?" the devil asked the man.

"Yep," the man replied, "Sure do."

"Well," the devil asked, "Aren't you afraid?"

"Nope," the man responded.

"Why not?" asked Satan.

The man said, "Why should I be scared of you? I've been married to your sister for 48 years."

Rules of the House

- Leftovers always expand to fill all available containers plus one.

- Three children plus two cookies equals one fight.

- The potential for disaster is in direct proportion to the number of TV remote controls divided by the number of viewers.

- The capacity of any hot water heater is equal to one and one-half sibling showers.

- The number of doors left open varies inversely with the outdoor temperature.

- The same clutter that will fill a one car garage will fill a two car garage.

- A newly washed window gathers dirt at double the speed of an unwashed window.

Timely T-Shirt

Seen on a T-shirt: "My Mother was a Travel Agent for Guilt Trips."

Who, You?

With profits from his food company, actor Paul Newman helped build a camp for critically ill children. It's called the Hole in the Wall Gang Camp, from Newman's movie *Butch Cassidy and the Sundance Kid.* Newman was sitting at a table one day with a camper who asked him who he was. The actor reached for a carton of Newman's Own lemonade and showed the boy his likeness on the container. "This is me," Newman said.

Wide-eyed, the camper asked, "Are you lost or something?" (Yale-New Haven Hospital Magazine)

NFL quarterback, Joe Montana, was unable to play for several weeks because of a hand injury. While having lunch with his family, a waitress said, "You poor thing! How did it happen?"

"I broke it playing football," Montana explained.

"Really?" replied the waitress. "Aren't you a little old to be playing football?" (Herb Caen, *San Francisco Chronicle*)

On his way to a reception held in his honor, Ulysses S. Grant got caught in a rainstorm and offered to share his umbrella with a stranger walking in the same direction. The man said he was going to Grant's reception out of curiosity; he had never seen the general.

"I have always thought that Grant was a much overrated man."

Grant replied, "That's my view also."

Epitaphs

Seen on the headstone of a dentist: "John Brown is filling his last cavity."

"Here lies John Yeast; Pardon me for not rising."

"Here lies the body of Jane Smith, wife of Thomas Smith, a marble cutter. This monument, erected as a tribute to her memory, may be duplicated for $250."

"He tried to make two jacks beat a pair of aces."

From the tombstone of a hypochondriac: "I told you I was sick."

In a church cemetery: "Remember friends as you pass by, As you are now, so once was I. So, as I am you soon will be, so prepare for death and follow me."

"Even though I walk through the valley of the shadow of death, I will fear no evil, for you are with me." (Psalm 23:4)

"Righteousness delivers from death." (Proverbs 10:2)

Mr. Perfect

After years of research, the profile of the perfect pastor has been developed. The perfect pastor preaches exactly fifteen minutes. He works from 8:00 am until midnight and is also the church janitor. He makes $100 a week, wears nice clothes, drives a new car, and gives $75 a week to the poor. He is 28 years old and has been preaching for 25 years. He is wonderfully gentle and handsome. He loves to work with teenagers and spends countless hours with senior citizens. He makes fifteen visits a day, spends eight hours a day in sermon preparation, and is always in the office when needed.

Penny Problem

In 1956, *Reader's Digest* sent out fifty million promotional letters with two pennies attached to each one. They depleted the entire New York area of pennies. The U.S. Mint had 60 million pennies shipped in to accommodate them. When the company got all of the pennies, they stored them all in one room. The floor collapsed under the weight of the coins.

Managerial Skills Test

The following quiz consists of four questions. It tells whether you are qualified for a management position. According to statistics, around 90% of the professionals failed the exam. The questions are not difficult. You just need to think.

1. How do you put a giraffe into a refrigerator?
Answer: Open the refrigerator. Put the giraffe in and close the door. (The above question tested whether you are doing simple things in a complicated way.)

2. How do you put an elephant into a refrigerator?
Wrong answer: Open the refrigerator. Put the elephant in and close the door.
Correct answer: Open the refrigerator. Take out the giraffe. Put the elephant in and close the door. (The above question tested your logic skills.)

3. The Lion King is hosting an animal conference. All the animals attend except one. Which animal does not attend?
Answer: The elephant. He's still in the refrigerator. (The above question tested your memory skills.)

4. There is a river where crocodiles live. How do you manage to cross it?
Answer: Simply swim through it. All the crocodiles are attending the animal conference. (The above question tested your comprehensive skills. If you did not get any of the questions right, congratulations! You are perfectly qualified for a management position.) (www.thebigshow.com)

Elementary Wisdom

A third-grade teacher asked her class to complete the beginning of some old-fashioned proverbs:

- Strike while the...bug is close.

- You can lead a horse to water...but how?

- Don't bite the hand that...looks dirty.

- A miss is as good as a...Mr.

- Better to be safe than...punch a fifth-grader.

- You can't teach an old dog...new math.

- The pen is mightier than the... pigs.

- A penny saved is... not much.

- If at first you don't succeed... get new batteries.

- When the blind leadeth the blind...get out of the way.

Parting Shot

A man died and the lawyer asked his widow, "What were your husband's last words?"

"Do you really need to know that?" the widow replied.

"Yes, I do," responded the lawyer.

"Well," the woman said, "The last thing I remember him saying was, 'You couldn't hit the broad side of a barn with that old gun.'"

Resignation

I am hereby officially tendering my resignation as an adult. I have decided I would like to accept the responsibilities of an 8-year-old again.

- I want to go to McDonald's and think it's a four-star restaurant.
- I want to sail sticks across a fresh mud puddle and make ripples with rocks.
- I want to think M&M's are better than money because you can eat them.
- I want to lie under a big oak tree and run a lemonade stand with my friends on a hot summer's day.

- I want to return to a time when life was simple. When all you knew were colors, multiplication tables, and nursery rhymes.
- I want to return to a time when all I knew was to be happy because I was unaware of all the things that should make me worried or upset.
- I want to think the world is fair and that everyone is honest and good.
- I want to believe that anything is possible.
- I want to be oblivious to the complexities of life and be overly excited by the little things again.
- I want to live simply again. I don't want my day to consist of computer crashes, mountains of paperwork, depressing news, how to survive more days in the month than there is money in the bank, doctor bills, gossip, illness, and loss of loved ones.
- I want to believe in the power of smiles, hugs, a kind word, truth, justice, peace, dreams, the imagination, mankind, and making angels in the snow.

So, I relinquish my checkbook, my car keys and my credit card bills. I officially resign from adulthood. (*FYI: Georgia Views and News*)

Whoops! Part 2

More mistakes that others have made that will make you feel better about yourself:

In 1897, the Remington Arms Company was offered the rights to a writing machine by the Wagner Typewriting Company. Remington turned it down saying, "No machine can replace an honest and reliable clerk." Wagner eventually became Underwood Typewriter Company and sold twelve million "writing machines."

In the 16th century, the Duke Lorenzo de Medici decided to paint over the old murals on his walls. Since then the Italian government has spent more than a million dollars trying to undo what the Duke had done. Those covered-over murals were originals by Leonardo da Vinci.

Newspaper columnist, Bill Kirby, tells of his sixth grade teacher who dated a guy in high school for a while but dropped him because he had no ambition. The fellow she ignored became a preacher named Billy Graham.

English Exam

If people from Poland are called Poles, why aren't people from Holland called Holes?

Why is the man who invests all your money called a broker?

Why are a wise man and a wise guy opposites?

Why do overlook and oversee mean opposite things?

If horrific means to be horrible, does terrific mean to be terrible?

Why isn't the number 11 pronounced "onety-one?"

Why do women wear evening gowns to nightclubs? Shouldn't they be wearing nightgowns?

If you take an Oriental person and spin him around several times, does he become disoriented?

When someone asks you, "a penny for your thoughts," and you put "your two cents in," what happens to the other penny?

If lawyers are disbarred and clergymen are defrocked, can electricians be delighted, musicians denoted, cowboys deranged, and dry cleaners depressed? (Bill Kirby, *The Augusta Chronicle*, 11/9/99)

Headlines
(Newspaper headlines that weren't proofread carefully)

"Patient at Death's Door; Doctors Pull Him Through"

"March Planned For Next August"

"Women's Movement Called More Broad-Based"

"Lawyers Give Poor Free Legal Advice"

"Juvenile Court to Try Shooting Defendant"

"Killer Sentenced to Die For Second Time in Ten Years"

"Twenty Year Friendship Ends at Altar"

Fairy Tales

A little girl asked her mom if all fairy tales begin with "Once upon a time." The mother replied, "No, dear. Most fairy tales begin with "If I'm elected..."

Food for Thought

The journey of a thousand miles begins with a broken fan belt and a leaky tire.

I used to be young and stupid. Now I can't even claim my youth as an excuse.

We are born naked, wet, and hungry. Then things get worse.

If you think nobody cares if you're alive, try missing a couple of car payments.

Employee Problems

The following are quotes supposedly taken from actual Federal Employee Performance Evaluations:

- When she opens her mouth, it seems that it is only to change feet.

- He sets low personal standards and then consistently fails to achieve them.

- This employee is depriving a village somewhere of an idiot.

- A gross ignoramus – 144 times worse than an ordinary ignoramus.

- He doesn't have ulcers, but he's a carrier.
- He brings a lot of joy whenever he leaves the room.

- If you see two people talking and one looks bored, he's the other one.

- If he were any more stupid, he'd have to be watered twice a week.

- If you give him a penny for his thoughts, you'd get change.

- Takes him 1½ hours to watch "60 Minutes."

Timely Questions

A bus station is where a bus stops. A train station is where a train stops. What is a workstation?

Do Lipton tea employees take coffee breaks?

Why do they put pictures of criminals up in the Post Office? Are we supposed to write to them? Why not put their picture on postage stamps so the mailmen can look for them while they deliver the mail?

If a man says something in the woods and there are no women there, is he still wrong?

Ever wonder what the speed of lightning would be if it didn't zigzag?

What do styrofoam manufacturers pack their product in for shipping?

Pyromania

A North Carolina man, having bought several expensive cigars, insured them against...get this...fire. After he had smoked them, he then decided that he had a claim against the insurance company and filed. The insurance company refused to pay, citing the obvious reason that the man had consumed the cigars normally. The man sued. The judge stated that since the company had insured the cigars against fire, they were obligated to pay. After the man accepted payment for his claim, the insurance company then had the man arrested – for arson. (*The Dispatch,* Volume 8 Issue 3)

In His Steps

A mother was preparing pancakes for her sons, Ryan and Kevin. The boys began to argue over who would get the first pancake. The mother said, "If Jesus were sitting here, he would say, 'Let my brother have the first pancake. I can wait.'"
Kevin turned to his brother and said, "Ryan, you be Jesus!"

More Timely Thoughts

It's amazing what you can accomplish with a little hard work and a lot of whining.

The older you get, the tougher it is to lose weight because your body and your fat are real good friends.

When my ship finally comes in, I'll probably be at the airport.
The best 10 years of a woman's life are between the ages of 29 and 30.

If at first you don't succeed, see if the loser gets anything.

Sometimes facing opportunity is like staring at the knees of a giraffe.

Anticipated Trip

Every time a boy saw his grandfather he'd say, "Make a sound like a frog, Grandpa." One day Grandpa asked, "Why?" "Because," said the boy, "Grandma said that when you croak we're going to Hawaii."

Deep Thoughts for Shallow Minds

Why does moisture ruin leather? Aren't cows outside most of the time? (Jerry Seinfeld, *SeinLanguage*)

Coming of Age

When you're twenty years old, you worry about what people think of you. When you're forty, you don't care what people think. When you're sixty, you discover that no one was thinking about you in the first place.

Long Wait

Joe, the newspaper reporter, had the unique opportunity to interview God. He asked the Lord, "Sir, what's a million years like to you?"

God replied, "Well, a million years to me would be like a second is to you."

Then Joe asked, "What's a million dollars like to you?"

God told him, "A million dollars? A million dollars would be to me as a penny is to you."

"Really?" Joe remarked. "Um, God, could I have a million dollars?"

"Sure, Joe," God responded, "In a second."

Bumper Stickers

- I didn't fight my way to the top of the food chain to be a vegetarian.
- Change is inevitable, except from a vending machine.
- Sometimes I wake up grumpy, other times I let him sleep.
- Warning: Dates in calendar are closer than they appear.

Annual Illness

"For all the advances in medicine, there is still no cure for the common birthday." (Senator John Glenn)

The Truth Hurts

Muhammad (The Greatest) Ali once allegedly refused to fasten his seat belt on an airplane. After repeated requests by the flight attendant to buckle up, Ali finally said, "Superman don't need no seat belt." The attendant replied, "Superman don't need no airplane."

Deep Thought

"Why is it that when we speak to God we are said to be praying, but when God speaks to us we are said to be schizophrenic?" (Lily Tomlin, *The Search for Signs of Intelligent Life in the Universe*)

Definition

Fisherman: A jerk on one end of a line waiting for a jerk on the other end of the line.

Proud Humility

A pastor was meeting his congregation at the front door at the end of a Sunday morning service. As usual, he was met by his parishioners commenting on his sermon. On this particular Sunday the message was on humility. One little lady came up to him and said, "You know, preacher, I've always been proud of my humility."

"God opposes the proud but gives grace to the humble." (James 4:6)

Overheard

"I don't suffer from insanity...I enjoy every minute of it."

"Make someone happy, mind your own business."

"If winners never quit and quitters never win, then how can you quit while you're ahead?"

"Those who can't laugh at themselves leave the job to others."

Strange but True

In 1990, the Wilkinsons, a family in Sussex, England received what they thought was a gift package of herbs from Australian relatives. They stirred the contents into a traditional Christmas pudding, ate half of it and put the remainder in the refrigerator.

Soon after, they heard from their Aunt Sheila that Uncle Eric had died. She wanted to know if they had received his ashes for burial in Britain.

The Wilkinsons quickly summoned their priest to bless and bury Uncle Eric's leftovers. (*The Wall Street Journal*, 12/18/90)

At age 47, the Rolling Stones' bass player, Bill Wyman, began a relationship with 13 year-old Mandy Smith, with her mother's blessings. Six years later, they were married, but the marriage only lasted a year. Not long after, Bill's 30 year-old son Stephen married Mandy's mother, age 46. That made Stephen a stepfather to his former stepmother. If Bill and Mandy had remained married, Stephen would have been his father's father-in-law and his own grandfather.

Quotable

"The human race has one really effective weapon, and that is laughter." (Mark Twain)

The World's Greatest Dog

A farmer had a neighbor who was a constant complainer. The farmer decided to impress this man for once in his existence, so he bought the world's greatest hunting dog. He invited his pessimistic neighbor to go hunting one day. The neighbor agreed.

He showed his neighbor how his dog could stand motionless for an hour and pick up a scent a mile away. No response from the neighbor.

Then, the farmer shot a duck, which landed in the middle of a pond. Upon command, the dog trotted out, walked on the water, retrieved the bird, and dropped him at the feet of his master.

"What do you think of that?" asked the farmer.

His friend replied, "Your dog can't swim, can he?"

A Picture of God

Art Linkletter saw a small boy drawing a picture. He inquired, "What are you drawing?" The boy replied, "A picture of God."

Linkletter told the boy that no one knows what God looks like, to which the boy confidently responded, "They will when I get through."

Jock Quotes

Basketball player Chris Washburn, commenting on his ability to drive to the basket, "I can go to my right and my left. That's because I'm amphibious."

"I'm going to graduate on time, no matter how long it takes." (Senior basketball player at the University of Pittsburgh)

"Nobody in football should be called a genius. A genius is a guy like Norman Einstein." (Joe Theismann)

"I play football. I'm not trying to be a professor. The tests don't seem to make sense to me, measuring your brain on stuff I haven't been through in school." (Ray Forsythe, Clemson football player)

"I've won at every level, except college and pro." (Shaquille O'Neal)

Shaquille O'Neal on whether he had visited the Parthenon during his visit to Greece: "I can't really remember the names of the clubs that we went to."

The Perfect Couple

Once upon a time, a perfect man and a perfect woman met. After a perfect courtship, they had a perfect wedding. Their life together was, of course, perfect.

One snowy, stormy Christmas Eve, they were driving their perfect car along a winding road, when they noticed someone at the side of the road in distress. Being the perfect couple, they stopped to help.

There stood Santa Claus with a huge bundle of toys. Not wanting to disappoint any children on the eve of Christmas, the perfect couple loaded Santa and his toys into their vehicle. Soon they were driving along delivering the toys.

Unfortunately, the driving conditions deteriorated and the perfect couple and Santa Claus had an accident. Only one of them survived the accident.

Who was the survivor? (The answer is on the next page.)

More Jock Quotes

"You guys line up alphabetically by height and you guys pair up in groups of three, then line up in a circle." (Bill Peterson, a Florida State football coach)

"He's a guy who gets up at six o'clock in the morning regardless of what time it is." (Lou Duva, boxing trainer, about boxer Andrew Golota)

NC State basketball player, Chuck Nevitt, explaining why he was late for practice, "My sister is expecting a baby, and I don't know if I'm going to be an uncle or an aunt."

Florida football coach, Steve Spurrier, telling Gator fans that a fire at Auburn's football dorm had destroyed all 20 books: "But the real tragedy was that fifteen hadn't been colored yet."

Headline Bloopers
(From newspaper headlines)

"Something Went Wrong in Jet Crash, Expert Says"

"Prostitutes Appeal to Pope"

"Two Sisters Reunited After 18 Years in Checkout Counter"

"If Strike Isn't Settled Quickly, It May Last a While"

"War Dims Hope for Peace"

"Four of Every Five Children Born in Cleveland is Born to a Single Woman"

"Couple Slain; Police Suspect Homicide" (James J. Kilpatrick, *The Writer's Art*)

Answer to The Perfect Couple

The perfect woman survived. She's the only one who really existed in the first place. Everyone knows there is no Santa Claus and there is no such thing as a perfect man. (Women stop reading here. Men should continue reading for the next answer.)

More Elevator Torture
(Things to do on an elevator.)

- Make explosion noises when anyone presses a button.

- Draw a little square on the floor with chalk and announce to the other passengers, "This is my personal space!'

- Stare at another passenger for a while, then announce in horror, "You're one of THEM!" and back away slowly.

- Crack open your briefcase or purse, and while peering inside, ask, "Got enough air in there?"

- Leave a box in the corner, and when someone gets on ask them if they hear something ticking.

Deep Thought

"The greatest job in the world is the professional wrestling referee. It's a sport with no rules of any kind. How do you screw that up?" (Jerry Seinfeld, *Seinlanguage*)

Words from Above

A magazine recently ran a "Dilbert quotes" contest. They were looking for quotes from real life Dilbert-type managers.

"What I need is a list of specific unknown problems we will encounter."

"E-mail is not to be used to pass on information or data. It should be used only for company business."

"This project is so important, we can't let things that are more important interfere with it."

"Teamwork is a lot of people doing what I say."

"We know that communication is a problem, but the company is not going to discuss it with the employees."

"Doing it right is no excuse for not meeting the schedule. No one will believe you solved this problem in one day! We've been working on it for months. Now, go act busy for a few weeks and I'll let you know when it's time to tell them."

The winner: "As of tomorrow, employees will only be able to access the building using individual security cards. Pictures will be taken next Wednesday and employees will receive their cards in two weeks." (*FYI: Georgia Views and News*)

Second Answer to The Perfect Couple

If there is no perfect man and no Santa Claus, the perfect woman must have been driving. This explains why there was an accident. By the way, if you're a woman and you're reading this, this illustrates another point: women never listen either. (*FYI: Georgia News and Views*)

Paid In Full

An eccentric man was on his deathbed. He had no family to take his inheritance. Besides, he wanted to take his money with him to the life beyond. He called his pastor, his doctor, and his lawyer to his bedside.

"I have a final request for you," he told his friends. "I am going to give each of you an envelope with $100,000. At my funeral, I want you to place the envelope in my casket before it is closed. That way, I can take my money with me."

A few days later the man died. The three men went by the casket for a final view and secretly slid the envelopes into the casket.

Several weeks later, the three men happened to see each other at a restaurant. The subject of their mutual friend's odd request came up when the pastor confessed, "I hate to admit it, fellas, but I kept $25,000 for our church's building fund."

The doctor also confessed, "I'm trying to build a new clinic for those in poverty and I kept $50,000."

The lawyer was shocked. "I can't believe you guys! You took that money without asking our dear friend?"

"Did you put all the money in the casket?" the other two asked.

"Of course," said the lawyer. "I deposited the money in my bank account and put a check in the envelope for the full amount."

Odd Titles

The following titles were included in *Bookseller* magazine's Odd Titles of the Year awards. These are real book titles.

"Fight Acne and Win"

"The Joy of Chickens"

"Proceedings of the Second International Workshop on Nude Mice"

"Scurvy Past and Present"

"Keeping Warm with an Axe"

"Detecting Fake Nazi Regalia"

"Gymnastics for Horses"

"Butchering Livestock at Home"

Millennial Myths
(Predictions about the year 2000)

"A trip down an air street to see a neighbor may be on top of an individual flying platform; a trip to Europe by rocket may take only half an hour." (The New York Times, 1967)

"Housewives will wash dirty dishes – right down the drain! Cheap plastic would melt in hot water." And homes will be waterproof, so "the housewife of 2000 can do her cleaning with a hose." (Popular Mechanics, 1950)

"We will press a button to formulate our clothing. We will have alternatives: what color, should it give off steam, do we want it to light up, do we want it to sparkle or do we prefer a matte finish, do we want it to glow in the dark, do we want an invisible shield?" (Betsy Johnson, fashion designer)

Going A Little Too Far

Some Elvis fans have always been a little extreme at times but a handful of the "King's" supporters have deified him in semiorganized services similar to some traditional forms of worship.

Martin Rush, a "minister" of the First Presleyterian Church in Denver, Colorado, says Elvis worship is spreading. The church has religious training, tent revivals, exorcisms, guitar lessons, and weight reduction classes.

At the Church of the Risen Elvis, also in Denver, they have enshrined a doll look-alike of Presley in an altar surrounded by candles and flowers. (Perucci Ferraiuolo, *Christianity Today*)

Grouchy Remarks
(Quotes from Groucho Marx)

"I've had a perfectly wonderful evening. But this wasn't it."

"I was married by a judge. I should have asked for the jury."

"Those are my principles. If you don't like them I have others."

"The husband who wants a perfect marriage should learn to keep his mouth shut and his checkbook open."

"The secret of success is honesty and fair dealing. If you can fake those, you've got it made."

Old Sayings

Old housewives never die – they just wash away.

Old janitors never die – they just kick the bucket.

Old golfers never die – they just lose their drive.

Old baseball players never die – they just strike out.

Old politicians never die – they just become devoted.

Old clerks never die – they just become defiled.

Old Masons never die – they just become dislodged.

Old dentists never die – they just lose their pull.

Old insurance agents never die – they just lose their premiums.

Old bankers never die – they just lose their balance.

Quotables

"Life is like a dogsled team. If you ain't the lead dog, the scenery never changes." (Lewis Grizzard)

"Cats are intended to teach us that not everything in nature has a function." (Garrison Keillor)

"I'm not a vegetarian because I love animals; I'm a vegetarian because I hate plants." (A. Whitney Brown)

For The Intellectual

Timely Words is proud to present the following tips for its redneck readers:

- While ears need to be cleaned regularly, this is a job that should be done in private using one's OWN truck keys.

- If you live alone, deodorant is a waste of good money.

- Always offer to bait your date's hook, especially on the first date.

- When approaching a four-way stop, the vehicle with the largest tires always has the right of way.

- Do not lay rubber while traveling in a funeral procession.

- If you have to vacuum the bed, it is time to change the sheets.

- Even if you're certain that you are included in the will, it is still considered tacky to drive a U-Haul to the funeral home.

- Refrain from talking to characters on the screen when attending a movie. Tests have proven they can't hear you.

No Respect
(More quotes from Rodney Dangerfield)

"I told my psychiatrist that everyone hates me. He said I was being ridiculous – everyone hasn't met me yet."

"My wife and I were happy for twenty years. Then we met."

Religious Icons

Mrs. Gray's first grade class was studying various cultures and religions. She asked the class to bring an item that was a well-known symbol of their particular religion.

That day, Mrs. Gray asked for volunteers in the class to share about their religious symbol. First, Abe stood up and said, "My family is Jewish so I brought a symbol that is meaningful to people of our faith – the Star of David."

"That's wonderful, Abe!" remarked his teacher. "Who would like to go next?"

Mary Elizabeth stood and said, "My family is Roman Catholic and the crucifix is meaningful to our faith." Mary Elizabeth passed the crucifix around for all to see.

"That's great, Mary Elizabeth," spoke Mrs. Gray.

Then Bubba stood up. "Mrs. Gray, I'd like to share my symbol with the class next. You see, my family is Baptist and what I brought is awful meaningful to our religion – a sweet potato casserole."

From Will Rogers...

"Even if you are on the right track, you'll get run over if you just sit there."

"There's no trick to being a humorist when you have the whole government working for you."

"Half our life is spent trying to find something to do with the time we have rushed through life trying to save."

"If you make any money, the government shoves you in the creek once a year with it in your pockets. All that don't get wet you can keep."

"If stupidity got us into this mess, why can't it get us out?"

"I belong to no organized party. I am a Democrat."

"You can't say civilizations don't advance...In every war they kill you a new way."

"We can't all be heroes because someone has to sit on the curb and clap as they go by."

Dumb Quotes

"Whenever I watch TV and see those poor starving kids all over the world, I can't help but cry. I mean I'd love to be skinny like that but not with all those flies and death and stuff." (Mariah Carey)

"I haven't committed a crime. What I did was fail to comply with the law." (David Dinkins, Mayor of New York, answering accusations that he failed to pay his taxes.)

"Smoking kills. If you're killed, you've lost a very important part of your life." (Brooke Shields)

"Outside of the killings, Washington has one of the lowest crime rates in the country." (Marion Barry, Mayor of Washington, D.C.)

"I've never had major knee surgery on any other part of my body." (Winston Bennett, University of Kentucky basketball player)

"The streets are safe in Philadelphia. It's only the people who make them unsafe." (Frank Rizzo, Mayor of Philadelphia)

Father Knows Best

A teenage boy had just earned his driver's license. His father made a deal with him. "If you bring your grades up, read your Bible everyday, and get your hair cut, I'll buy you a car."

After a few months, the boy said, "Dad, can I have a car now?" The father responded, "Son, I've been real proud of you.

You've got your grades up and you've been reading your Bible like we agreed. But you haven't cut your hair."

The boy said, "I've been thinking about that...you know, Moses and Samson and Jesus had long hair."

"Yes," said the father, "And they walked everywhere they went."

That's What It's All About

There was a great loss recently in the entertainment world when Larry LaPrise, the Detroit native who wrote the song "Hokey Pokey" died. The funeral home had trouble keeping the body in the casket. They'd put his left leg in and he'd put his left leg out and...well, you know the rest. (*FYI: Georgia Views and News*)

Twenty Sayings We'd Like to See on Those Office Inspirational Posters

1. Rome did not create a great empire by having meetings...they did it by killing all those who opposed them.

2. Eagles may soar, but weasels don't get sucked into jet engines.

3. TEAMWORK...means never having to take all the blame yourself.

4. The beatings will continue until morale improves.

5. Hang in there, retirement is only thirty years away!

6. When the going gets tough, the tough take a coffee break.

7. Aim Low...Reach Your Goals...Avoid Disappointment (*FYI: Georgia Views and News*)

More Words to Live By

"Always remember you are unique, just like everyone else."

"If you lend someone $20, and never see that person again, it was probably worth it."

"Duct tape is like the force. It has a light side and a dark side and it holds the universe together."

"Experience is something you don't get until just after you need it."